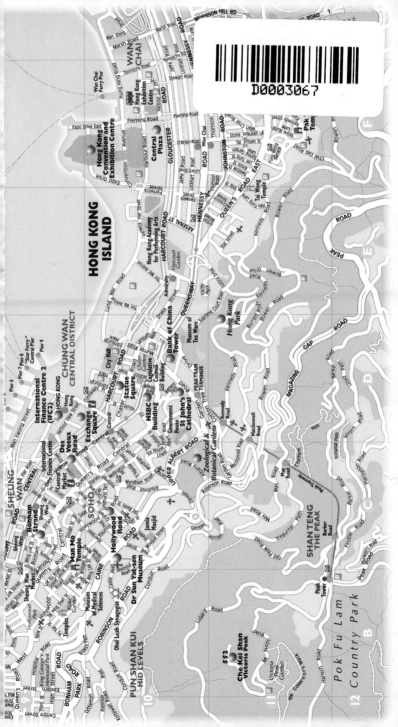

Hong Kong's
25Best

by Joseph Levy Sheehan

Fodor's Travel Publications
New York • Toronto
London • Sydney • Auckland
www.fodors.com

How to Use This Book

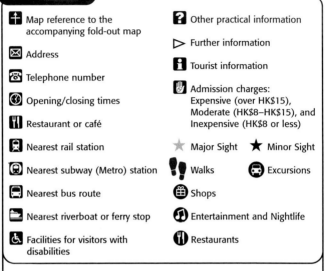

KEY TO SYMBOLS

🗺	Map reference to the accompanying fold-out map	❓	Other practical information
✉	Address	▷	Further information
☎	Telephone number	ℹ	Tourist information
🕐	Opening/closing times	✋	Admission charges: Expensive (over HK$15), Moderate (HK$8–HK$15), and Inexpensive (HK$8 or less)
🍴	Restaurant or café		
🚉	Nearest rail station	★	Major Sight / Minor Sight
Ⓜ	Nearest subway (Metro) station	👣	Walks
🚌	Nearest bus route	🚐	Excursions
⛴	Nearest riverboat or ferry stop	🛍	Shops
♿	Facilities for visitors with disabilities	🎭	Entertainment and Nightlife
		🍽	Restaurants

This guide is divided into four sections

• **Essential Hong Kong:** An introduction to the city and tips on making the most of your stay.

• **Hong Kong by Area:** We've broken the city into four areas, and recommended the best sights, shops, entertainment venues, nightlife and restaurants in each one. Suggested walks help you to explore on foot.

• **Where to Stay:** The best hotels, whether you're looking for luxury, budget or something in between.

• **Need to Know:** The info you need to make your trip run smoothly, including getting about by public transport, weather tips, emergency phone numbers and useful websites.

Navigation In the Hong Kong by Area chapter, we've given each area its own tint, which is also used on the locator maps throughout the book and the map on the inside front cover.

Maps The fold-out map accompanying this book is a comprehensive street plan of central Hong Kong. The grid on this map is the same as the grid on the Hong Kong Island and Kowloon area locator maps and has upper case grid references. Sights and listings within the New Territories area have lower case grid references.

Contents

Introducing Hong Kong

Hong Kong is the city where East and West meet. It's a mixture of macho capitalism and religion; backstreets and gleaming skyscrapers; wild country-side and manicured urban parks – plus designer shops, posh restaurants, nightclubs and chic bars

Hong Kong has had a turbulent ride since the British sailed away in 1997. At first, as well as economic uncertainty, there were huge population shifts: Many Hong Kongers who could claim passports or immigration rights got out and Chinese who wanted a new life and a degree of political freedom moved in. Then, in the early years of the new century, bird flu and SARS drove the tourists away faster than you could say Special Administrative Region.

Add on the political mess the British left behind them and the rapid economic development of other Chinese cities, drawing industry away from Hong Kong, and things looked shaky for a time. The massive investment of the new airport looked fit to bring the whole economic house of cards tumbling, but Hong Kong has now rebranded itself as one of the most dynamic economies and cultures in the world, and especially a great destination for tourists. The SARS outbreak of 2003 caused a serious rethinking of how to bring the tourists back. Hotel and restaurant prices fell to competitive levels and new sights have sprung up, such as Hong Kong Disneyland and the developments around the Po Lin Monastery.

Hong Kongers are a special breed—tough, hard working, resilient. They embrace Western ideas but traditional Chinese culture is strong. You'll see people in the parks practising tai chi, the ancient, elegant exercise routines as often as you'll see a squash game or joggers. The Special Administrative Region of Hong Kong has had a difficult first decade, but the difficulties it has faced have only made it stronger.

Facts + Figures

- Hong Kong has a population of 7 million.
- 80 percent of Hong Kong's territory is rural or country park.
- The Tian Tin Buddha at Po Lin Monastery on Lantau Island is the world's largest seated bronze Buddha.

SARS

In 2003 fears about bird flu gave way under the world panic caused by another disease, Severe Acute Respiratory Syndrome, (confusingly with the same initials as Special Administrative Region). The territory disinfected everything it could, took everyone's temperature daily, closed schools and handed out face masks. The pandemic was averted.

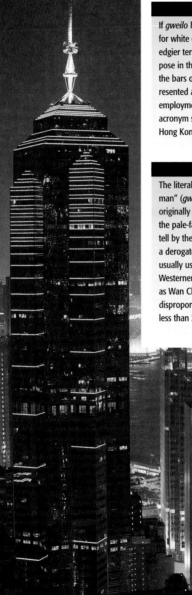

FILTH

If *gweilo* has become an acceptable term for white office workers, FILTH is a slightly edgier term. It describes Europeans who pose in their business suits after work in the bars of Lan Kwai Fong and who are resented a little for their excellent terms of employment and frequent paid leave. The acronym stands for Failed In London, Try Hong Kong.

GWEILOS

The literal translation for *gweilo* is "ghost man" (*gweipor* means "ghost woman"), originally coined as a derogatory label for the pale-faced colonial masters. You can tell by the tone of voice if it is still meant in a derogatory manner, but nowadays it is usually used as a general reference for Westerners, whose presence in areas such as Wan Chai, especially at night, seems disproportionate given that they constitute less than 2 percent of the population.

A Short Stay in Hong Kong

DAY 1

Morning After a buffet breakfast in your hotel head straight for the **Peak** (▷ 38–39) taking the Peak tram to view the city and its islands stretched out before you. Go to the viewing deck at the top of the Peak Tower for 360-degree views over the city.

Mid-morning Back down in Central head for **Cat Street** (▷ 44) where antiques and bric-a-brac fill the markets; load up with gifts and curiosities.

Lunch Enjoy a value set lunch at one of the trendy diners along Elgin Street.

Afternoon What better way to experience the real Hong Kong than to take a ride on the **Star Ferry** (▷ 60–61) to Kowloon where you can indulge in a little retail therapy in the streets around Canton Road and the adjacent malls.

Mid-afternoon For a break from shopping, try afternoon tea at the **InterContinental** lobby lounge (▷ 112) with its spectacular views of the harbor and quiet luxury.

Dinner Before dinner make sure you're at the clock tower at 8pm to watch the nightly **Symphony of Lights** (▷ 62–63), which lights up the harbor. For dinner, if you have managed to get a reservation go back to the island and try **Caprice** (▷ 48) where the superb cuisine will give you an experience you'll remember for a long time to come.

Evening Take the Mid Levels escalator (an experience in itself) to Soho for a few drinks in **Staunton's Wine Bar** (▷ 47). Then to Lan Kwai Fong for some fun at **Coconuts** (▷ 46) or one of the many other bars.

DAY 2

Morning Take the MTR Tung Chung line to **Lantau Island** (▷ 98–99). Here the first fun of the day begins with a 30-minute cable-car ride on Skyrail. Enjoy 360-degree views before arriving at Ngong Ping Village, where you can wander around the outlets, experience the tea-drinking ceremony, watch a funny monkey movie and learn about the Buddha.

Mid-morning Walk over to the **Tian Tan Buddha** (▷ 98–99), buy a meal coupon at the bottom of the stairs and head up to the Buddha and the museum inside.

Lunch Enjoy a vegetarian lunch at the **monastery** (▷ 98–99), or if you must eat meat hop back down to Ngong Ping to try the food outlets there.

Afternoon Head to Kowloon and make your way to **Ladies Market** in Mong Kok (▷ 68), where you can try your hand at bargaining and load up with inexpensive clothes. Take in Nelson Street Wetmarket where you will never believe some of the items on sale in buckets and on slabs.

Mid-afternoon Don't forget to seek out the bird market in Yuen Po Street where you can watch the caged birds sing while their owners feed them crickets with chopsticks.

Dinner This time the area to choose has to be **Mong Kok** (▷ 68) for a real Chinese dinner. Try **Fu Wah** (▷ 75) in Viceroy Market, which comes highly recommended as one of the best inexpensive pork and rice restaurants in the city.

Evening Knutsford Terrace is the place for you, as there are bars to suit all tastes and a quieter, more local atmosphere than Soho or Lan Kwai Fong.

▼ **Aberdeen (▷ 24–25)**
▼ Visit one of the many
▼ floating restaurants in
Aberdeen's harbor.

Botanical and Zoological Gardens (▷ 26–27)
Escape from the city in this paradise of flora and fauna.

Central Plaza (▷ 28)
Enjoy bird's eye views from the 44th-floor observation point.

Cheung Chau Island (▷ 94–95) Explore the hills and temples of "Long Island."

Exchange Square (▷ 29)
Admire the buildings, statues and fountains.

Hong Kong Disneyland (▷ 96–97) New fairy-tale theme park on Lantau Island.

Hong Kong Park (▷ 30)
Birds, lakes, plants and waterfalls spread over 25 acres (10ha).

Hong Kong Wetland Park (▷ 80–81) 151 acres (61ha) of natural and landscaped parklands.

Kowloon Walled City Park (▷ 54) An oasis of calm in central Kowloon.

Man Mo Temple (▷ 31)
Hong Kong's oldest temple, dedicated to Man and Mo.

Museum of Art (▷ 55)
Among the works on display is the first known painting of Hong Kong.

Museum of History (▷ 56) Exhibits trace Hong Kong's history.

Ocean Park (▷ 32–33)
One of southeast Asia's largest amusement parks.

Po Lin Buddha and Lantau Island (▷ 98–99) Giant bronze Buddha atop a mountain at Po Lin.

Science Museum (▷ 57)
Robots, virtual reality and lots more hands-on science projects.

Space Museum (▷ 58–59) Don't miss seeing an Omnimax film here.

Stanley (▷ 34–35)
Famous market, as well as beaches and temples.

Star Ferry (▷ 60–61)
Operating since 1898, this ferry ride is a "must do."

Symphony of Lights (▷ 62–63) Stunning light show in Victoria Harbour.

Temple Street (▷ 64) ▼
Market stands selling ▼
almost everything. ▼

Ten Thousand Buddhas Temple (▷ 82–83) So named due to the sheer number of Buddha statues within.

University Museum and Art Gallery (▷ 36–37)
A hidden gem with a fine collection of Chinese antiquities.

Victoria Peak (▷ 38–39)
Take the tram to the top of the Peak for amazing views.

Waterfront Promenade (▷ 65) By night or day some of the most stunning cityscapes in the world.

Wong Tai Sin Temple (▷ 84) Vast temple complex with gardens.

These pages are a quick guide to the Top 25, which are described in more detail later. Here they are listed alphabetically and the tinted background shows the area they are in.

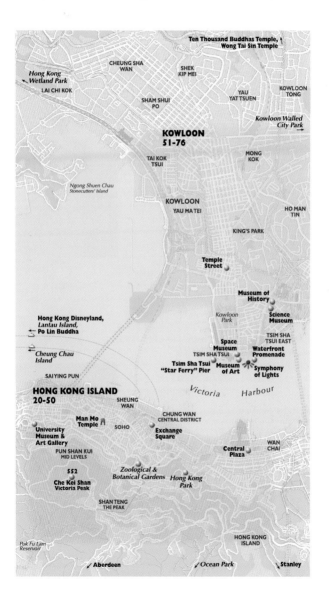

Ten Thousand Buddhas Temple,
Wong Tai Sin Temple

CHEUNG SHA
WAN

SHEK
KIP MEI

*Hong Kong
Wetland Park*

LAI CHI KOK

YAU
YAT TSUEN

KOWLOON
TONG

SHAM SHUI
PO

*Kowloon Walled
City Park*

**KOWLOON
51-76**

TAI KOK
TSUI

MONG
KOK

*Ngong Shuen Chau
Stonecutters' Island*

KOWLOON
YAU MA TEI

HO MAN
TIN

KING'S PARK

Temple
Street

Museum of
History

*Hong Kong Disneyland,
Lantau Island,
Po Lin Buddha*

*Kowloon
Park*

Science
Museum

*Cheung Chau
Island*

Space
Museum
TSIM SHA TSUI

TSIM SHA
TSUI EAST

Waterfront
Promenade

SAI YING PUN

Tsim Sha Tsui
"Star Ferry" Pier

Museum
of Art

Symphony
of Lights

**HONG KONG ISLAND
20-50**

SHEUNG
WAN

Victoria   Harbour

University
Museum &
Art Gallery

Man Mo
Temple

SOHO

CHUNG WAN
CENTRAL DISTRICT

Exchange
Square

PUN SHAN KUI
MID LEVELS

WAN
CHAI

Central
Plaza

$$2
Che Kei Shan
Victoria Peak

Zoological &
Botanical Gardens

Hong Kong
Park

SHAN TENG
THE PEAK

*Pok Fu Lam
Reservoir*

HONG KONG
ISLAND

Aberdeen

Ocean Park

Stanley

Shopping

A huge part of the fun of a trip to Hong Kong is shopping. Among locals it is a way of life rather than a trip to get necessities. The whole family will visit one of the shopping centers to enjoy the food halls, the air-conditioning and the experience of planning their next purchase. For visitors there are the many craft items to carry home as souvenirs, but another reason to shop in Hong Kong is that many items such as cameras, electronics, clothes, shoes and glasses can be cheaper here than in Europe. American visitors might pick up a few bargains, too, but if you want to buy something be aware of the price at home. Be aware also, that on large new items you may be charged import duties on your return home and there is the inconvenience of getting things back damaged.

Emporia and Flea Markets

The most popular items with visitors are in the big Chinese emporia and flea markets. Look out for hand-embroidered silk shawls and blouses, Chinese slippers, all kinds of silk cushion covers and bedspreads. There are lots of tailors in Hong Kong who can make suits or shirts within a few days at relatively inexpensive prices. For bargain hunters there are many factory shops and outlets, where all kinds of seconds and

From traditional Chinese products to international designer stores, Hong Kong has it all

BARGAINING

Bargaining is an essential part of the shopping skills of the Hong Konger. They are of little use in department stores or other fixed-price establishments but in the markets or smaller shops bargaining is essential.

A good idea when bargaining is to know roughly how much the item costs in a fixed-price shop and aim to conclude a deal at a slightly lower price than that. Try a few practice bargains first to get the hang of it and be aware that, especially in highly touristy areas, the trader may assume you have no idea of the value of an item and ask for far too much on the off chance that you'll fall for it.

end-of-run clothes are available at a fraction of the retail price. However, these places need some determined assessing and you should be prepared for bad days when there is little worth buying. Another serious contender for your vacation funds is jewelry, either made with semiprecious stones or cloisonné, or the really expensive stuff made with diamonds and precious stones. Gold jewelry is beautifully made, often using Chinese characters as a design feature. Hong Kong is a great place to buy jade and the tourist board organizes an hour-long seminar on how to look for the best jade. Flea markets, such as Cat Street (Upper Lascar Row), offer Mao memorabilia, posters, jewelry and many more knickknacks.

Chinese Specialties

Ceramics are also an excellent purchase with both Chinese and Western dinner services, teapots in handmade basket cozies and abstract pottery. Chinese cooking utensils are inexpensive to buy in the wetmarkets and are very useful and visually interesting. Also attractive are bamboo steaming baskets for vegetables and tiffin carriers—stacked metal containers for carrying your lunch to work. Inexpensive and difficult to get outside of Chinese communities are Chinese dried goods and herbal remedies such as ginseng, dried fish such as abalone and shark's fin, and even birds' nests. Chinese tea is also a good buy. Kites and wooden toys are excellent, too, and there are crafts from other parts of Asia that are also reasonably priced.

SAFE SHOPPING

The Hong Kong Tourist Board, no doubt fed up with tourist complaints about rip-offs, has produced an excellent booklet called *A Guide to Quality Shops and Restaurants,* which lists all the places that have qualified under its scheme called QTS. It's a little hefty to stick in your handbag but it is very useful if you intend to do some serious shopping.

Shopping by Theme

Whether you're looking for a department store, a quirky boutique, or something in between, you'll find it all in Hong Kong. On this page shops are listed by theme. For a more detailed write-up, see the individual listings in Hong Kong by Area.

ANTIQUES

Arch Angel Antiques (▷ 44)
Cat Street Galleries (▷ 44)
Honeychurch Antiques
   (▷ 44)
Karin Weber Antiques
   (▷ 45)

ARTS AND CRAFTS

The Banyan Tree Ltd.
   (▷ 44)
Mountain Folkcraft (▷ 45)
Vincent Sum Designs
   (▷ 45)

CHINESE EMPORIA

Chinese Arts and Crafts
   (HK) Ltd. (▷ 44, 70)
Yue Hwa Chinese Products
   Emporium (▷ 71)

COMPUTERS

Computer Mall (▷ 44)
Mong Kok Computer
   Centre (▷ 71)

ELECTRONICS

Broadway Photo Supply
   (▷ 70)
Fortress (▷ 70)

JEWELRY

Anita Chan Jewellery
   (▷ 70)
Chow Tai Fook (▷ 44)
Elissa Cohen Jewellery
   (▷ 70)
Just Gold (▷ 70)
Larry Jewelry (▷ 45)
Opal Mine (▷ 71)
Tse Sui Luen Jewellery
   International (▷ 71)

MEN'S CLOTHES

Sam's (▷ 71)
W. W. Chan & Sons (▷ 71)

SHOPPING AREAS AND MALLS

Causeway Bay (▷ 44)
Lo Wu Commercial City
   (▷ 106)

Ngong Ping Village
   (▷ 106)
Ocean Centre (▷ 71)
Pacific Place (▷ 45)
Rise Commercial Building
   (▷ 71)
Sha Tin (▷ 89)

STREET MARKETS

Jardine's Bazaar (▷ 44)
Li Yuen Street Market
   (▷ 45)
Marble Road Market
   (▷ 45)
Tai Po Market (▷ 89)
Upper Lascar Row (Cat
   Street, ▷ 45)

WOMEN'S CLOTHES

Fa Yuen Street (▷ 70)
Factory Outlets (▷ 70)
Lan Kwai Fong (▷ 45)
Pedder Building (▷ 45)

Hong Kong by Night

The place to be in Hong Kong for a good time at night is Hong Kong Island and in particular Lan Kwai Fong. It is an area of older buildings, once pretty sleazy but now clean, pedestrian-only and full of expensive watering holes. Its bars will be full of young men and women, wearied from a day's money-making in front of the office monitor, and refreshed again by lager and cocktails.

Relaxing
To the east, the district of Wan Chai was traditionally the base for sleazy clubs during the days of the Vietnam war. It is slightly more respectable now, with hostess bars charging an arm and a leg for a beer, but also some good clubs and bars. Wan Chai is home to some relaxed pubs if all you're after is a quiet drink.

Party with the Locals
Kowloon also offers places to drink especially in the touristy Tsim Sha Tsui (TST) where there are hostess bars and clubs around Knutsford Terrace as well as a couple of good places for a relatively inexpensive drink. The area is a little run down these days, but if you want to mingle with locals without a trip out to the New Territories this is the place to do it. Bars generally open around midday and close after 2am, while clubs open from around 6pm until around 1am on weekdays and as late as 4am on weekends.

There are plenty of bars, clubs and restaurants to try in Hong Kong

---

HOSTESS CLUBS

Hong Kong developed a racy reputation in the 1960s and 70s when it became popular with American soldiers. Though sleaze is now fairly well hidden, there are some traces of Hong Kong's lurid side in the hostess clubs. These are mainly concentrated in TST and Wan Chai where customers may inadvertently find themselves on the wrong end of a huge bill. Be warned. Though advertised drink prices may sound reasonable, customers may be charged for merely talking to one of the scantily clad service staff.

Eating Out

Hong Kong has the highest per capita ratio of restaurants in the world. Along with shopping, eating is another favorite pastime. Although the city is famed for its Cantonese cuisine, it also has many international and fusion restaurants.

Cantonese Cuisine
Typical Cantonese dishes include crab in black bean sauce, steamed fish, shrimp with chili sauce, roast pigeon and fried noodles with beef. Meals are often accompanied by Chinese tea, the three basic types being green, black and oolong. Needless to say, milk and sugar aren't required.

Where to Eat
Restaurants in the more expensive hotels serve high quality cuisine, while restaurants on the outlying islands tend to specialize in seafood. Street vendors, though no longer so prevalent, sell a variety of reasonably priced snacks, such as fish balls, noodles and roast chestnuts. If you are feeling brave you can forgo the bigger places and try out your chopstick skills (▷ 50) in one of the tiny street cafés selling pork and rice or dim sum (▷ 48).

Opening Hours
Restaurants usually open for lunch around 11.30am, closing at 3pm and opening again for dinner between 6 and 11pm. A 10 percent service charge is often added to the bill in the smarter restaurants, while tips aren't expected in cheaper local restaurants.

AFFERNOON TEA

The red pillar boxes have all been repainted green, but the British ritual of afternoon tea is still going strong. For the full works–china, chandeliers and chamber music– the Peninsula Hotel in Salisbury Road is hard to beat, but the Grand Hyatt in Wan Chai (▷ 112) and the Mandarin Oriental (▷ 112) are worthy (and equally expensive) alternatives.

Hong Kongers love to eat and the island has both Cantonese and international restaurants to choose from

Restaurants by Cuisine

There are restaurants to suit all tastes and budgets in Hong Kong. On this page they are listed by cuisine. For a more detailed description of each restaurant, see Hong Kong by Area.

AMERICAN AND MEXICAN

Al's Diner (▷ 48)
The Bostonian (▷ 74)
!Caramba (▷ 49)
Coyote (▷ 49)
Dan Ryan's Chicago Grill (▷ 74)
Mezzo Grill (▷ 76)

CANTONESE

Fu Wah (▷ 75)
Hang Fook Lau (▷ 49)
Jumbo Floating Restaurant (▷ 49)
Long Island (▷ 106)
Man Wah Restaurant (▷ 50)
Tung Yee Heen (▷ 106)
Yan Toh Heen (▷ 76)
Yung Kee Restaurant (▷ 50)

EUROPEAN

360 at the Shangri-La 360 (▷ 106)
Bulldog's Bar and Grill (▷ 74)
Caprice (▷ 48)
Jimmy's Kitchen (▷ 49, 75)
Lobster Bar and Grill (▷ 50)
Santa Lucia Restaurant and Lounge (▷ 76)

FRENCH

Amigo Restaurant (▷ 48)
Brasserie Le Fauchon (▷ 48)
Brasserie on the Eighth (▷ 48)
Gaddi's (▷ 75)
Le Tire Bouchon (▷ 50)

INDIAN

The Ashoka Restaurant (▷ 48)
The Curry Pot (▷ 49)
Delhi Club Mess (▷ 74)
Gaylord Indian Restaurant (▷ 75)
Khyber Pass (▷ 75)
Tandoor Restaurant (▷ 50)
Woodlands International Restaurant (▷ 76)

ITALIAN

Anthony's Catch (▷ 90)
Cammino (▷ 48)
Chef (▷ 49)
Fat Angelo's (▷ 74)
The Mistral (▷ 76)
Nadaman (▷ 76)

JAPANESE

Aqua Roma & Aqua Tokyo (▷ 74)
Sagano Restaurant (▷ 76)
Sakurada (▷ 90)
Tokio Joe (▷ 50)

PAN-ASIAN

Chung Shing Thai Restaurant (▷ 90)
Cosmopolitan Curry House (▷ 90)
Felix (▷ 74)
Golden Siam Thai Cuisine (▷ 106)
Heaven on Earth (▷ 75)
Indochine 129 (▷ 49)
Jimmy Wong's Kitchen and Café (▷ 90)
Nam San Gok (▷ 90)
Peak Café (▷ 50)
Tung Kee Seafood Restaurant (▷ 90)

SPANISH

Boca (▷ 48)
El Cid (▷ 74)
La Comida (▷ 49)

If You Like…

However you'd like to spend your time in Hong Kong, these top suggestions should help you tailor your ideal visit. Each sight or listing has a fuller write-up elsewhere in the book.

ISLAND HOPPING

Spend a day at Cheung Chau (▷ 94) walking and lazing on the beach.
Get away from traffic on Lamma (▷ 100) with its seafood restaurants, bars and beaches.
Soar above Lantau (▷ 98) on the shiny Skyrail cable-car and see the giant Buddha.
Take a trip out to tiny Po Toi (▷ 101) for challenging walks, great views and rock carvings.

PAMPERING

Soothe away all your stress with a mudbath and massage at the Four Seasons Spa (▷ 46).
Have an underwater massage at Chuan Spa (▷ 73) in Mong Kok.
Try the reflexology and aromatherapy, then have a sauna at the Island Shangri-La (▷ 112).
Spend your whole visit at the Plateau Spa accommodations at the Grand Hyatt (▷ 112).

Spa pampering (above) and retail therapy (below)

SHOPPING MALLS

Indulge in a little retail therapy at the Ocean Centre (▷ 71).
Wander for hours without seeing daylight in Pacific Place (▷ 45).
Experience suburban shopping in the warrens of New Town Plaza, Sha Tin (▷ 89).

SKYSCRAPERS

Tell the time using the roof of Central Plaza (▷ 28).
Check out the inside-out Hong Kong & Shanghai Banking Corporation Building (▷ 41).
Wonder at the stylish 70-story Bank of China Tower (▷ 40) with its mixture of Ming dynasty and ultramodern design.

Skyscrapers of Central district (right)

Browsing the Stanley Market; Man Mo Temple (below)

MARKETS

Take the bus out to Stanley (▷ 34) where the market fills the town.

Refresh your wardrobe with inexpensive clothes at the Ladies Market (▷ 68).

Bargain for antiques, Mao memorabilia and other kitsch curiosities and bric-a-brac at Upper Lascar Row (▷ 45).

Buy a piece of jade, try the seafood and buy some goodies at Temple Street Night Market (▷ 64).

TEMPLES

Meet gods Man and Mo at the colorful Man Mo Temple (▷ 31).

Have your fortune told by a professional at the huge Wong Tai Sin Temple (▷ 84).

Count the Buddha statues at the Ten Thousand Buddhas Temple (▷ 82).

Visit one of the temples dedicated to Tin Hau, the goddess of seafarers. Try the one in Stanley (▷ 34).

PARTYING

Hong Kong nightlife (above)

Revel the night away in the Wan Chai's district's hedonistic bars and clubs (▷ 47).

Hang out with *gweilos* at Bahama Mama's (▷ 73).

Enjoy the after-work vibe at La Dolce Vita (▷ 46).

Experience the real Hong Konger's nightlife in Hillwood Road (▷ 69), Kowloon.

ROOMS WITH A VIEW

Request a harbor-view room at the InterContinental (▷ 112).

Gaze over the harbor scene from the center of the island waterfront at the Grand Hyatt (▷ 112).

Peer down over skyscraper roofs from the Island Shangri-La tower (▷ 112).

A luxurious harbor-view room at the Shangri-La (left)

STROLLS IN THE PARK

Check out the beautiful but artificial splendors of
Hong Kong Park (▷ 30).

See trees, plants and animals from
around the world at the Botanical
and Zoological Gardens (▷ 26).

Admire the statue avenue, bird life
and landscaped ponds of Kowloon
Park (▷ 67).

Enjoy the remains of the notorious
Kowloon Walled City in Kowloon
Walled City Park (▷ 54).

*The Botanical and
Zoological Gardens
(below)*

USING CHOPSTICKS

Exercise your digits at the
Jumbo Palace Floating
Restaurant (▷ 49).

Grapple with street food at a
dai pai dong (▷ panel, 49).

Seize some traditional Cantonese
cuisine at Yung Kee Restaurant (▷ 50).

ENTERTAINING THE KIDS

See the pandas and enjoy the rides at Ocean
Park (▷ 32).

Meet the leopards and orangutans at the
Zoological Gardens (▷ 26).

Take a sampan ride round Aberdeen Harbour
(▷ 24).

Press the knobs at the interactive Space
Museum (▷ 58).

WHAT'S FREE

Climb to the top of the Peak and admire the
amazing views from Lugard Road (▷ 38).

Enjoy the exhibits at the University
Museum and Art Gallery (▷ 36).

Goggle at the Symphony of Lights
(▷ 62).

Ride the escalator to the Mid Levels.

Spend a day at Silverstrand beach
(▷ 89).

*Chinese bowl and
chopsticks; a sea lion
at Ocean Park (above)*

View from the Peak (right)

Hong Kong by Area

From shopping malls to sandy beaches, temples to theme parks, haute cuisine to dim sum, and designer labels to souvenirs, Hong Kong Island has it all. There's nowhere so fast, furious and fun.

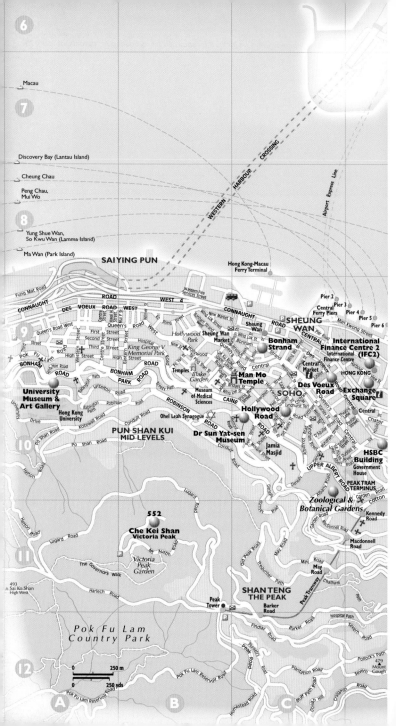

Macau

Discovery Bay (Lantau Island)

Cheung Chau

Peng Chau,
Mui Wo

Yung Shue Wan,
So Kwu Wan (Lamma Island)

Ma Wan (Park Island)

SAI YING PUN

Hong Kong-Macau
Ferry Terminal

WESTERN HARBOUR CROSSING

Airport Express Line

Fung Mat Road

CONNAUGHT ROAD

DES VOEUX ROAD WEST

Western Fire
Services Street

Pier 2

Central
Ferry Piers

Pier 3

Pier 4

Pier 5

Pier 6

Queen's Road West

First Street

Second Street

Third Street

High Street

Hospital

King George V
Memorial Park

New Market St

Sheung Wan
Market

CONNAUGHT ROAD

SHEUNG WAN

**International
Finance Centre 2
(IFC2)**

International
Finance Centre

Queen's Road

BONHAM

BONHAM PARK ROAD

Hollywood
Park

Temples

Blake
Garden

Museum
of Medical
Sciences

**Bonham
Strand**

**Man Mo
Temple**

Central Market

**Central's
Market**

HONG KONG

Des Voeux Road

SOHO

**Exchange
Square**

**University
Museum &
Art Gallery**

Hong Kong
University

Robinson Road

Ohel Leah Synagogue

CAINE ROAD

**Hollywood
Road**

Chater

Central

Po Shan Road

Kotewall Road

Conduit Road

**PUN SHAN KUI
MID LEVELS**

**Dr Sun Yat-sen
Museum**

**Jamia
Masjid**

Conduit Road

UPPER ALBERT ROAD

**HSBC
Building**

Government
House

Hatton Road

Po Shan Road

Lugard Road

Albany Road

**PEAK TRAM
TERMINUS**

**Zoological &
Botanical Gardens**

Garden Road

Kennedy
Road

552

**Che Kei Shan
Victoria Peak**

Victoria
Peak
Garden

Macdonnell Road

Macdonnell
Road

493
Sai Ko Shan
High West

The Governor's Walk

Lugard Road

Harlech Road

**SHAN TENG
THE PEAK**

May Road

Chatham

Peak Tramway

**Pok Fu Lam
Country Park**

Peak
Tower

Barker
Road

Findlay Road

Hospital Path

Severn Road

479
Mount
Gough

Plantation Road

Pollock's Path

0   250 m

0   250 yds

Pok Fu Lam Reservoir Road

Homestead Road

Peak Road

Severn Road

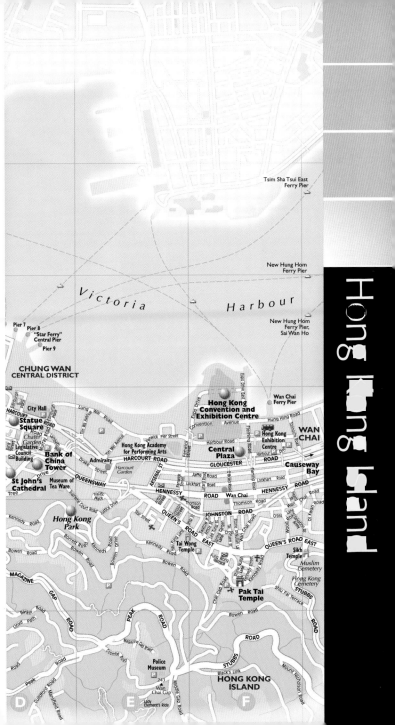

Aberdeen

JUMBO FLOATING RESTAURANT

HIGHLIGHTS

● Dinner at the Jumbo
Floating Restaurant (▷ 49)
● A sampan ride around the
harbor
● Views over the harbor
from the Chinese cemetery
above the town

TIP

● Ap Lei Chau has become a
hot spot of outlets where
anything from last year's
designer clothing at knock-
down prices, to furniture and
antiques can be found.

**Before the British arrived, Aberdeen was
a small fishing village, full of pirates and
smugglers. Today the pirates are gone,
but fishing remains the livelihood of
many families.**

Fragrant Harbor Aberdeen is known in Chinese
as Heung Gong Tsai, meaning "little fragrant harbor"; this name is thought to have derived from
the village's trade in sandalwood and incense pro-
duction. The whole of the Special Administrative
Region (SAR) is now described by this term, Hong
Kong. The chief draw of a visit to Aberdeen, which
is actually the second largest urban area in the
SAR, is to visit the harbor, where for centuries
families have lived out their lives on houseboats
all moored tightly together. At the western end of
the harbor is the wholesale fish market.

Aberdeen Harbour is full of life, being home to a large fishing fleet and hundreds of people living on junks. It is renowned for its floating restaurants, of which the most famous is the Jumbo Floating Restaurant—with a staff of more than 300

Highlights A highlight of your visit is to negotiate with one of the savvy old ladies that ply tourists around the harbor. Take a trip out to Ap Lei Chau (around HK$50), a tiny island just offshore (either by junk or via the more mundane road that links the island with Aberdeen). Wooden junks have been built on this island for centuries and occasionally a few still are. Back in Aberdeen, the Tin Hau Temple in Reservoir Road, dedicated to the goddess of the sea, is worth a look, followed by a walk uphill to the huge cemetery with views over the harbor.

Floating restaurants There are two mega-restaurants in Aberdeen Harbour catering to the vast numbers of people who come out here to eat the seafood as a tourist experience. Free ferry rides take customers out to the restaurants.

THE BASICS

+ See map ▷ 92–93
✉ Aberdeen
🍴 Jumbo Floating Restaurant, one other floating restaurants, bars and cafés in town
🚌 7 from Central Bus Station, 70 from Exchange Square
♿ Few
🚤 Sampan boats: inexpensive

Botanical and Zoological Gardens

HIGHLIGHTS

● Bromeliads, air plants and carnivorous plants
● Amazing variety of butterflies, especially in fall
● Jaguar
● Orangutan families
● Tree kangaroos from central New Guinea
● Flamingos
● Golden lion tamarins

In the middle of the urban sprawl these gardens form a quiet haven of peace. In fall, the scents of flowers fill the air and the wings of myriad butterflies shimmer in the light with a dazzling hue.

Oasis of calm This century-old complex, which once looked out over Victoria Harbour, is enclosed today by the city's towers (and bisected by a road; use the underpass to get from one part to the other). There are hundreds of species of birds, including many rare ones that breed happily in captivity. In the greenhouse are air plants, bromeliads and insectivorous plants such as pitcher plants, Venus fly-traps and rare butterworts. Early in the morning the gardens are full of people performing the slow exercise program known as t'ai chi ch'uan, which is designed to get the life

There are more than 1,000 plant species in the Botanical Gardens, while the zoo successfully bred three endangered ring-tailed lemurs in March 2006 (far left)

forces flowing properly around the body. The zoo, though small, is surprisingly comprehensive and has a number of endangered species. The zoo specializes in primates and has orangutans from Sabah and golden lion tamarins from South America.

Government House Opposite the gardens is Government House, where Hong Kong's British governors used to live. The house was built in 1855 and was added to through the years, perhaps one of the most attractive additions being the Japanese tower and roof corners that were put up during the Occupation. Government House is closed to the public, but you can peer through the gates or, if you are lucky, visit its gardens when they open for two days in March, when the azaleas are in bloom.

THE BASICS

www.lcsd.gov.hk/parks

✚ C10

✉ Several entrances; from Central the most accessible gate is on Upper Albert Road

☎ Botanic Gardens: 2530 0154. Government House: 2530 2003

🕐 Gardens, zoo, aviaries: daily 6am–7pm (Fountain terrace garden until 10pm). Greenhouses: 9–4.30

Ⓢ Central

🚌 3B, 12, 13 from Central; 12A, 12M, 40M from Admiralty

🍴 Snack kiosk

♿ Good

🎟 Free

27

Central Plaza

THE BASICS

www.centralplaza.com.hk

🏠 F10

✉ 18 Harbour Road, Wan Chai

☎ 2586 8111

🍴 Nearby cafés

Ⓠ Wan Chai

♿ Good

👆 Free

HIGHLIGHTS

● Brooding neoclassical grandeur of interior
● Artwork in the lobby
● Quiet spot in forecourt outside the building
● Views from the 46th floor

Completed in 1992, Central Plaza was, for a few years, Hong Kong's tallest building. It rises to 78 floors and stands at 1,227ft (374m)—counting the spire.

Majestic It's not often an office block is included in a list of tourist destinations, but this one certainly deserves a visit for its stunning architecture and for the views from the observation point on the 46th floor. Confusingly located in Wan Chai, (you'd think it would be in Central with a name like that) the building looks from a distance like a huge glass prism with its triangular shape and acres of plate glass. The top of the reinforced concrete building forms a clock with four different color neon panels changing their configuration every 15 minutes. Considered by some to be overdecorated, the sheer glass walls include the design, in gold, of the outline of a smaller building. Downstairs at ground level is a tiny garden, which is good for a quiet moment in the surrounding urban chaos. From here an escalator leads up to the wide public piazza filled with exotic plants forming a public access bridge across Wan Chai.

Highest church The building was actually meant to be taller than it is but an economic downturn during its construction led to a reduction in height. It may now even make the top five tallest buildings in China, but Central Plaza is blessed by being the home of the highest church in the world: it sits on the top office floor below the huge glass atrium.

Life-size water buffalo (below right) and the escalators at Exchange Square (below)

Exchange Square

The best times to visit this square and the surrounding areas are when they are busy—either at lunchtime when the people who work nearby are out getting their lunch, or on Sunday when the Filipina maids on their day off are picnicking with their friends.

The scene Exchange Square, designed by Hong Kong's P&T Architects in 1985, consists of three ultramodern tower blocks, including the Hong Kong Stock Exchange, linked to a series of overhead walkways to Sheung Wan district in the west. The square contains some of Central's more elegantly designed structures. The towers provide shade, the waterfalls the cooling sound of water, the statuary a sense of dignity and place. It can be a chilly spot, with brisk winds blowing in straight from the sea and channeled through the gaps between the buildings. The grand buildings are huge slabs of smooth pink granite, quarried locally in Hong Kong. The three monolithic statues in the square are *Oval with Points* by Henry Moore, *Water Buffaloes* by Dame Elizabeth Frink and the stunning tai chi ch'uan practitioner by Ju Ming.

Number 1 Take a look inside No. 1 Exchange Square. On the first floor you will find an exhibition gallery; the trip up the escalator takes you past another two stunning waterfalls. The overall effect of the square is very bleak. The scene is, however, considerably more cheerful on Sunday when the place is full of high-pitched noise and laughter and the picnickers fill every available spot.

THE BASICS

✚ D9
✉ Exchange Square, Central
🍴 Café in the Forum; also fast food available on lower floors
🚇 Central
♿ Good

HIGHLIGHTS

● Life-size bronze water buffalo statues
● Oversized statue of t'ai chi ch'uan practitioner
● Waterfront
● Henry Moore statue *Oval with Points*
● No. 1 Exchange Square

Hong Kong Park

TOP 25

Plants and birds in the aviary at Hong Kong Park

THE BASICS

✚ D11

✉ Main entrance: Supreme Court Road, Central. Nearest entrance to Museum of Teaware: Cotton Tree Drive, Central

☎ Museum: 2869 0690

🕐 Park: 6.30am–11pm. Museum: Wed–Mon 10–5. Aviary and Conservatory 9am–5pm. Closed 24–25 Dec, 1 Jan, and first 3 days of Chinese New Year

🍴 Café/bar in park

Ⓜ Admiralty

🚌 12, 23B, 33, 40, 103; get off at first stop in Cotton Tree Drive

♿ Good

🆓 Free

In a space-deprived Hong Kong, this modern little park is a joy. Instead of roses or ancient trees you'll find man-made waterfalls, concrete pools and paths around the grass and flowers, all for a sense of harmony and balance.

Artificial paradise Hong Kong Park is a small miracle of artificiality. Its architects used what little original landscape existed and built the park into the contours of the hillside. It's fun to walk past the pools filled with koi carp or through the Edward Youde Aviary where tree-high walkways take you cheek by bill with brilliantly plumaged tropical birds.

The conservatory The Forsgate conservatory is a huge building. It has three separate sections—display plants, humid plants and dry plants—which take up a large chunk of the entire park . Adjustable climate control equipment simulates conditions from disparate climate regions. The varieties of bamboo are particularly impressive.

Refreshments old and new The Museum of Teaware in Flagstaff House, the oldest colonial building in Hong Kong, deserves a look. Flagstaff House is a charming piece of mid-19th century architecture, and the exhibition of teapots and the like brings out the collector in almost everyone. Most afternoons the park is full of elegantly dressed parties posing for wedding photos, having just emerged from the registry office, which is in the park.

HIGHLIGHTS

● Walk-in aviary
● Artificial waterfalls
● Conservatory
● Flagstaff House and Museum of Teaware
● Observation tower
● Bonsai trees in tai chi garden

Man Mo Temple

The altar (below) and incense coils of Man Mo (below right)

The most remarkable aspects of this tiny, but historic temple is the canopy of incense coils which create a heady, mysterious atmosphere.

Taoism The temple, built in 1847, is one of the oldest surviving structures on Hong Kong Island and looks rather bullied by the soaring apartment blocks that surround it. It is dedicated to two Taoist deities who represent the pen and the sword. These are Man, or Man Cheong, the god of literature; and Mo, or Kuan Ti, the god of war. The statues of Man and Mo are dressed lavishly in beautifully embroidered outfits. Beside the two main statues in the temple are representations of Pao Kung, the god of justice, and Shing Wong, the god who protects this region of the city. By the door are the figures of some lesser deities. A drum and a gong are sounded whenever an offering is made to the gods. The atmosphere seems almost casual—cats wander around, fortune-tellers divine the future using *chim* (numbered bamboo sticks), and visitors place offerings of fruit or incense sticks in the offering boxes next to the statues inside the temple.

Nearby sights Next door, to the right, is the Litt Shing Kung, or All Saints Temple. Here, too, you can see people consulting the resident soothsayers, who interpret the *chim* tipped out of bamboo pots. In the courtyard of the temple stand gilded plaques, carried in processions, while inside are the two 1862 sedan chairs used to convey the figures of the two gods.

THE BASICS

➕ C9
✉ Junction of Hollywood Road and Ladder Street
🕐 Daily 8–6
🚇 Sheung Wan
♿ Access difficult
🎟 Free

HIGHLIGHTS

● Statues of Man Cheong and Kuan Ti
● Sedan chairs once used to carry the statues
● Embroideries surrounding the statues
● Drum and bell on right of entrance door
● Soot-blackened deities on left of entrance door
● Gold and brass standards carried during parades
● Resident fortune-tellers

Ocean Park

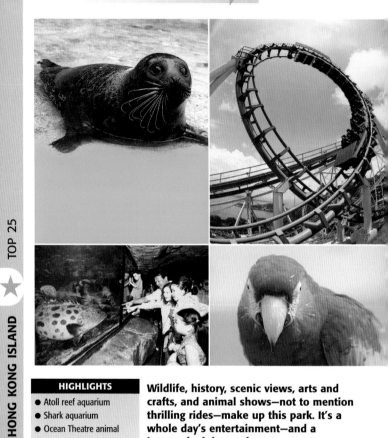

HIGHLIGHTS

- Atoll reef aquarium
- Shark aquarium
- Ocean Theatre animal shows
- Raging River flume ride
- Le Le and Ying Ying
- Bird shows
- Dragon Ride

TIPS

- Avoid the weekends when things get very crowded.
- If the weather is a little wild the cable-car ride may be closed down.

Wildlife, history, scenic views, arts and crafts, and animal shows—not to mention thrilling rides—make up this park. It's a whole day's entertainment—and a jam-packed day at that.

Thrills galore There is so much to see and do at this park that it takes a little time to plan your visit. So start by finding out the times and locations of the animal shows; then organize the rest of your day around them.

Aerial view Most fun of all, perhaps, is the cable-car trip into the park. You dangle in a fragile little car, stopping and starting for no apparent reason as the wind whistles around and under you, with the sea gently boiling below. To come out of the park you take a 745-ft long (227m) escalator ride.

What to see The Lowland Gardens are home to two giant pandas (Le Le and Ying Ying were gifts from the mainland in 2007 to celebrate 10 years since reunification), a motion simulation ride and the bird show. Marine Land has three exhibits, the scariest being the enormous jellyfish, while the 35 species of shark are always engaging. In this sector is the Ocean Park Tower, which hoists its passengers sedately up a 236ft (72m) pole and rotates them for some spectacular views.

Rides Two areas of rides, Adventure Land and Headland Rides, offer all the stomach-churning excitement you could ever ask for and there is a special area designed for small children. Finally, there's Bird Paradise, a huge walk-in aviary with some endangered species living among all the wild birds.

THE BASICS

www.oceanpark.com.hk
+ See map ▷ 92–93
✉ Ocean Park Road, Aberdeen
☎ 2552 0291
🕐 Daily 10–6
🍴 Fast-food, Bayview Restaurant Terrace Café
🚍 41A, 70, 90, 97 from Central Bus Terminus. Ocean Park Citibus leaves from Admiralty MTR every 10 min
♿ Excellent
💲 Expensive
❓ Height restrictions on some rides

Stanley

SIZE: 1
2. 4 : $50-
6. 8 : $70-
10. 12. 14 : $80-

HIGHLIGHTS

● Views from bus to Stanley
● Tin Hau Temple
● Stanley Beach
● St. Stephen's Beach
● Stanley Military Cemetery
● Stanley Market
● Kuan Yin Temple

TIPS

● A 15-minute walk along Wong Ma Kok Road is a signpost down to the much nicer St. Stephen's Beach.
● Check out the Correctional Services Museum at 45 Tung Tau Wan Road (Tue–Sun 10–5). Admission is free.

The most stunning thing about a visit to Stanley, in the south of Hong Kong Island, is the journey there. Get an upstairs seat on the double-decker bus— the ride is as good as any at Ocean Park.

Temples Most visitors come to Stanley for its market, but the village has many other attractions. Close to the market is the Tin Hau Temple, first built on this spot in the early 1700s. The bell and drum are said to have belonged to a famous pirate, Cheung Po-Tsai. The bell was cast in 1767, and it is thought that the pirate used it to send messages to his ships. The temple also contains the skin of a tiger, shot in Stanley in 1942. Farther along the road is a second temple, dedicated to Kuan Yin, goddess of mercy. Some claim to have seen the 20ft (6m) statue of the goddess move.

Visit Stanley for its market, beaches, temple and maritime museum, or just for a walk along the seafront

Beaches and the market The beach at Stanley is a good one, and a short bus ride farther along takes you to St. Stephen's Beach, where there is a graveyard for all the soldiers who have died in Hong Kong since Britain claimed the island as a colony. Although now rather touristy, the famous market is quite good, with linen shops as well as stands selling clothes made in other Asian countries. Stanley is the stepping-off point for Po Toi Island (▷ 101), an hour's ferry ride away, but worth the trip for the prehistoric rock carvings and a good beach for swimming.

Stanley is also an increasingly hip diving destination. The three-story Murray House on the seafront houses some great restaurants as well as the Hong Kong Maritime Museum. Murray House was built in 1846—in Central. It was moved to Stanley in 1998.

THE BASICS

- See map ▷ 92–93
- Market: 10.30–6.30. Temple: 6–6
- Restaurants and pub food in Stanley Main Street
- 6, 260 from Exchange Square
- Ferries to Po Toi depart Sat, Sun only 10.30, 11.30
- Excellent

University Museum and Art Gallery

- Nestorian bronze crosses
- Bronze mirrors
- Neolithic black pottery cup
- Pottery horse, Western Han dynasty
- Qing dynasty woodcarving
- Bronze drum
- Sui dynasty spittoons
- Indian Buddhist sculptures
- Modern Chinese pottery from Jinghdezhen and Shiwan

This interesting collection of pre-dominantly Chinese objects is worth the effort to see it. The museum is on the University of Hong Kong campus and is usually blessedly empty.

Nestorian bronze crosses The exhibits in this out-of-the-way museum, in the university's Fung Ping Shan Building, date from the 5th century BC onward, but the highlight is a set of 467 Nestorian bronze crosses—the largest such collection in the world—which belonged to a Christian sect that originated in Syria and came to China during the Tang dynasty (AD618–906). The crosses date back to the Yuan dynasty (1280–1367) and were probably worn as part of a belt or as a pendant. They were made in various cross-shapes, including swastikas, birds and conventional crucifixes.

- The Tea Gallery serves tea in the traditional style: Mon–Sat 10–5, Sun 2–5.

Since its foundation in 1953, the University Museum has amassed over 1,000 Chinese antiquities including bronze rice sculptures, a globe and wooden shutters (below)

Ceramics and bronzes Notable among the other bronze items on display are mirrors from the Warring States period (475–221BC), and Shang and Zhou ritual vessels and weapons. The museum also houses an enormous collection of ceramics dating back as far as neolithic times. The neolithic pottery is very fine, and the Han dynasty horse is full of life. Look for the three-color glaze Tang pottery, the famous kiln wares from the Song dynasty and the polychrome ceramics from the Ming and Qing dynasties.

Beyond Hong Kong Objects from other Asian countries include some Indian Buddhist sculptures and items from Thailand, Vietnam and Korea. Scroll paintings, inlaid blackwood furniture and a huge bronze drum make up the rest of the collection.

THE BASICS

www.hku.hk/hkumag
🔢 A9
✉ 94 Bonham Road
☎ 2241 5500
🕐 Mon–Sat 9.30–6, Sun 1–6. Closed public holidays
🚇 Sheung Wan
🚌 3B from Jardine House on Connaught Road or 23, 40, 40M from Pacific Place, Admiralty
♿ None
🖐 Free

Victoria Peak

- Views over Hong Kong
- Tram ride to the top
- Old Governor's Lodge, with toposcope in its gardens
- Souvenirs in Peak Galleria
- Outdoor tables in Peak Café (▷ 50)
- Green-arrowed walk up Mount Austin Road

- If you can, make your trip to the Peak on a clear day.
- Take a picnic and do the walk around the Peak.

Visiting the Peak is one of the first things to do when you get to Hong Kong. At 1,811ft (552m) the hilltop views are spectacular and the area offers some peaceful, shady walks.

Head for heights Some people like to make the pilgrimage up the Peak twice—once during the day and again at night to see the city lights. The Peak is a relatively unspoiled oasis in a concrete jungle, home of the rich and a good place for a quiet walk or even a jog. The circular walk around the peak via Lugard and Harlech roads takes less than an hour and offers jaw-dropping views that surpass the purpose-built viewing platforms.

Top stop The Peak Tower was given a makeover in 2005 and now offers multiple distractions, from

The best thing about the Peak is its breathtaking views over the city. Visit both during the day and after dark. The Peak Tower (bottom middle) was designed by British architect Terry Farrell in the shape of an upheld rice bowl

Madame Tussauds to a virtual reality games room and touristy shops. From the viewing platform at the top of the building are spectacular panoramas over the city. The nearby Peak Galleria has further distractions to offer such as the computerized fountain and lots more shops and cafés.

View from the top The trip up in the Peak Tram, constructed in 1888, is good fun as long as you don't have to line up for hours—avoid weekends and the first day after a misty spell. Feeding dollars into one of the telescopes is also worthwhile on a clear day. From the tram stop you can walk along Mount Austin Road to Victoria Park Gardens and the ruins of the Governor's Lodge, destroyed by the Japanese in World War II. A noticeboard outside the Peak Tower shows the walk routes, which take about an hour with photo stops.

THE BASICS

www.thepeak.com.hk
✚ B11
✉ Peak Tower, Peak Road
🕓 Peak Tram: runs 7am–midnight
🍴 Peak Galleria (snacks) and Peak Café
🚌 Trams run every 10–15 min from terminals at Garden Road and Cotton Tree Drive. Central Bus 15C from Central Bus Terminal to Victoria Gap. 125 from Admiralty to lower tram terminus
♿ Good
💰 Tram fare: moderate. Peak Tower: free

More to See

BANK OF CHINA TOWER

Designed by the Chinese-American architect, I. M. Pei, and built between 1985 and 1990, this 984-ft (300m) high, 70-floor tower dominates the Hong Kong skyline. The building soars upward in a series of triangles toward a prism at the top. Amazingly, it is built with no internal supporting columns.

✚ D10 ✉ No. 1 Garden Road, Central
🕒 Mon–Fri 8–6 🚇 Central ♿ Free

BONHAM STRAND

Ginseng shops, antiques markets and tiny lanes with ancient shops now abound on the road where the British first set foot. Despite the renovations this area still recalls the old Hong Kong and many of the old ways still hang on.

✚ C9 ✉ Bonham Strand, Sheung Wan
🕒 Shops close on public holidays, particularly Chinese New Year 🍴 Food stalls in Sheung Wan Market and streets around Bonham Strand; fast food near MTR station
🚇 Sheung Wan 🚃 Trams stop at Western Market and go on through Central to Causeway Bay ♿ Good ♿ Free

CAUSEWAY BAY

This district is famous for youth chic and rowdy local restaurants. It's particularly fun at night. It's home to the excellent Central Library as well as Happy Valley Racecourse.

✚ H9 🍴 Many 🚇 Causeway Bay
♿ Good

DES VOEUX ROAD

Named after a 19th-century governor of the island, Sir William Des Voeux, this is one of Hong Kong Island's main streets and is lined with company headquarters, such as the Hong Kong & Shanghai Banking Corporation Building (▷ opposite).

✚ C9 🚇 Sheung Wan ♿ Good

DR SUN YAT-SEN MUSEUM

The arrival of a Sun Yat-Sen museum in Hong Kong almost feels like confirmation that Hong Kong is back in mainland hands. The revered nationalist leader has museums dedicated to him in almost every major Chinese city, but this one really stands out, both in terms of the architecture, and

Early morning tai chi in Victoria Park, Causeway Bay

the two excellent permanent exhibitions. It's in the 1914 Kom Tong Hall, a stunning four-story mansion.
🔲 C10 ▣ 7 Castle Road, Mid Levels, Central ☎ 2367 6373 ⏰ Mon–Wed and Fri–Sat 10–6, Sun 10–7 💰 Inexpensive

HOLLYWOOD ROAD

If you are a serious antiques collector or just like browsing among junk and curios, a major destination on your itinerary has to be Hollywood Road. The antiques shops start at the beginning of the road and continue for about 1 mile (1.6km), incorporating Upper Lascar Row, which is a real flea market (▷ 45). Antiques that are more than 100 years old must have a certificate of authenticity. If you plan on spending a lot, you might want to check with your consulate first to find out if there will be duty charges. The importation and exportation of raw or worked ivory is governed by strict rules. It's best to check with customs officials to find out what paperwork is required to export ivory.
🔲 C10 ⏰ Sheung Wan ♿ Poor

HONG KONG CONVENTION & EXHIBITION CENTRE (HKCEC)

The once bland Convention & Exhibition Centre, originally built in 1988 on reclaimed land, underwent extensive expansion in 1997. The new structure has made an iconic impact on the Island's waterfront, being easily identified as the gargantuan spaceship-like building protruding into the harbor. The linked towers of the HKCEC contain two of the Island's most prestigious hotels—the Grand Hyatt (▷ 112) and the Renaissance Harbour View.

A second expansion started in July 2006, due for completion in 2009.
🔲 F10 ▣ 1 Convention Avenue, Wan Chai ☎ 2582 8888 ⏰ Wan Chai 💰 Free

HONG KONG & SHANGHAI BANKING CORPORATION (HSBC) BUILDING

This 1985 building, designed by British architect Sir Norman Foster and prefabricated in several different continents at a cost of over US$1 billion, looks as if it's been turned inside out.

A food store on Des Voeux Road

The Bank of China Tower

The supporting structures appear on the outside, all mechanical parts are exposed, and many walls are glass.
✚ D10 ⊠ Des Voeux Road/Statue Square, Central 🚇 Central 💷 Free

IFC 2

With true Chinese engineering panache, IFC 2 obliterated Hong Kong's skyscraper height record when it opened in 2003 and now stands proudly above the pack from its 88-story perch close to the Star Ferry terminal. This sail-shape beauty, designed by Cesar Pelli has no mass-market tourist access, but the Hong Kong Monetary Authority (HKMA) has an information area on the 55th floor. You might have to pretend you're interested in liquidity preferences, but the view is great. There's a luxury shopping mall at the base of the building (and the Airport Express station is in the basement).
✚ D9 ⊠ 1 Harbour View Street, Central

HKMA Info Centre
☎ 2878 1111; www.hkma.gov.hk
🕐 Mon–Fri 10–6, Sat 10–1 💷 Free

REPULSE BAY

The pretty beach here gets very crowded on public holidays and on weekends, but there is a temple and a modern shopping arcade too.
✚ See map ▷ 92–93 🚌 6, 61 from Central Bus Terminus

ST. JOHN'S CATHEDRAL

This Anglican church, a relic of British colonialism, has stood since 1849. The dominant feature inside is the stained-glass representation of the crucifixion. The church can be found below the Lower Peak tram terminal on Garden Road.
✚ D10 ⊠ 4-8 Garden Road ☎ 2523 4157
🕐 7–6 🚇 Central ♿ None

STATUE SQUARE

Statue Square is just one section of a whole chain of pleasant open spaces. The space here allows for amazing views of the towering landmarks of modern architecture all around you.
✚ D10 ⊠ Statue Square, Central
🚇 Central 🚋 Trams to Causeway Bay and Sheung Wan ♿ Excellent 💷 Free

The pretty beach at Repulse Bay

A statue of Sir Thomas Jackson Bart in Statue Square

An Island Walk

This inner city walk passes shops selling all manner of strange herbal remedies, then continues along famous Hollywood Road to Soho.

DISTANCE: 1.6 miles (2.5km) **ALLOW:** 1.5 hours

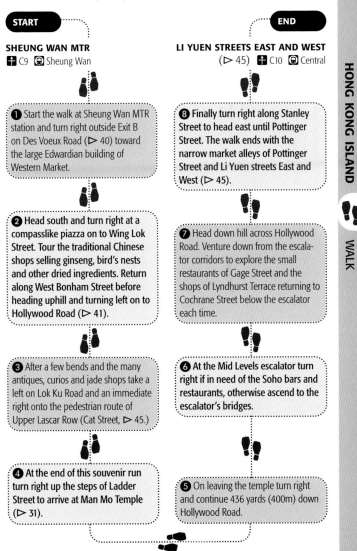

START

SHEUNG WAN MTR
✚ C9 🚇 Sheung Wan

END

LI YUEN STREETS EAST AND WEST
(▷ 45) ✚ C10 🚇 Central

1 Start the walk at Sheung Wan MTR station and turn right outside Exit B on Des Voeux Road (▷ 40) toward the large Edwardian building of Western Market.

8 Finally turn right along Stanley Street to head east until Pottinger Street. The walk ends with the narrow market alleys of Pottinger Street and Li Yuen streets East and West (▷ 45).

2 Head south and turn right at a compasslike piazza on to Wing Lok Street. Tour the traditional Chinese shops selling ginseng, bird's nests and other dried ingredients. Return along West Bonham Street before heading uphill and turning left on to Hollywood Road (▷ 41).

7 Head down hill across Hollywood Road. Venture down from the escalator corridors to explore the small restaurants of Gage Street and the shops of Lyndhurst Terrace returning to Cochrane Street below the escalator each time.

3 After a few bends and the many antiques, curios and jade shops take a left on Lok Ku Road and an immediate right onto the pedestrian route of Upper Lascar Row (Cat Street, ▷ 45.)

6 At the Mid Levels escalator turn right if in need of the Soho bars and restaurants, otherwise ascend to the escalator's bridges.

4 At the end of this souvenir run turn right up the steps of Ladder Street to arrive at Man Mo Temple (▷ 31).

5 On leaving the temple turn right and continue 436 yards (400m) down Hollywood Road.

Shopping

ARCH ANGEL ANTIQUES

Huge antiques shop with floors of antique ceramics, professionally restored furniture, sculpture and art. They also deal in smaller pieces for the passing trade. Close by is their sister shop Arch Angel Art, which specializes in modern Vietnamese paintings.

➕ C10 ✉ 53–55 Hollywood Road, Central ☎ 2851 6848 ◉ Daily 9.30–6.30 Ⓜ Central

THE BANYAN TREE LTD.

Antiques, arts, crafts and furniture from India, the Philippines, Indonesia and South America. A branch in the Repulse Bay shopping arcade.

➕ D10 ✉ 214–218 Prince's Building, Chater Road, Central ☎ 2523 5561 ◉ Mon–Sat 10.30–7, Sun 12.30–7 Ⓜ Central

CAT STREET GALLERIES

This shopping complex full of antiques dealers and curio shops is close to the Hollywood Road antiques area.

➕ B9 ✉ 38 Lok Ku Road, Sheung Wan ☎ 2541 8908 ◉ Mon–Fri 11–6, Sat 10–6 Ⓜ Sheung Wan

CAUSEWAY BAY

This is a major shopping area, less touristy than Central or Tsim Sha Tsui. Here is the enormous Times Square mall and four Japanese department stores—Matsuzakaya, Mitsukoshi, Daimaru and Sogo—all with several designer outlets. You'll also find Marks & Spencer, all the local chain stores and Lane Crawford, a classy Southeast Asian department store.

➕ G10 Ⓜ Causeway Bay

CHINESE ARTS AND CRAFTS (HK) LTD.

Compared to other Chinese emporia, this one stocks more designer rosewood and lacquer furniture, lamps and carpets. You can find some pretty valuable pieces here.

➕ F10 ✉ Lower Block, China Resources Building, 26 Harbour Road, Wan Chai ☎ 2827 6667 ◉ Daily 10.30–7.30 Ⓜ Wan Chai

---

SHOPPING TIPS

Before parting with any money check whether the warranty is an international one or just for Asia. If it is the latter, the price should be lower. Always check a quote with other retailers before making a substantial purchase. When buying software, make sure you know the specs of your hardware and check the minimum memory and speed requirements on the box before you buy. Prices in Hong Kong are comparable to those in the US; Europeans will find some good bargains.

CHOW TAI FOOK

This is just one of a good local jewelry chain that has branches in Causeway Bay, Central and around Mong Kok. Checkout the jade and watch the way local people go about the serious business of buying.

➕ C10 ✉ G2 Aon China Building, Queen's Road, Central ☎ 2523 7128 ◉ Daily 10–8 Ⓜ Central

COMPUTER MALL

A collection of specialist computer shops retailing hardware and software. Stores look more sophisticated than those in Sham Shui Po, but the selection is basically the same.

➕ H10 ✉ 11th–12th floors, The In Square, Windsor House, 311 Gloucester Road, Causeway Bay ◉ Daily 11–8.30 Ⓜ Causeway Bay

HONEYCHURCH ANTIQUES

Browse here for antique silver, utensils, jewelry and a collection of ornaments from around the world.

➕ C10 ✉ 29 Hollywood Road, Central ☎ 2543 2433 ◉ Mon–Sat 10–6 Ⓜ Central

JARDINE'S BAZAAR

This is one of Hong Kong's oldest street markets, full of food shops, good shops selling clothes and handbags, and excellent bargains in inexpensive clothes.

➕ H10 ✉ Jardine's Bazaar and Jardine's Crescent,

Causeway Bay 🕐 Daily
mid-morning to late
🚇 Causeway Bay

KARIN WEBER ANTIQUES
Here you'll find a mixture of arts and crafts, modern Asian pieces and Chinese country antiques.
➕ C10 ✉ Ground floor 20 Aberdeen Street, Central
☎ 2544 5004 🕐 Mon–Sat 11–7, Sun 1–6 🚇 Central

LAN KWAI FONG
Several boutiques and shops sell clothes at reduced prices in this area, notably CCC, Gat and Whispers; all stock some well-known names at good prices.
➕ C10 ✉ Central 🚇 Central

LARRY JEWELRY
One of several branches of the internationally famous jeweler.
➕ E10 ✉ Shop 232, Level 2, The Mall, Pacific Place Two, 88 Queensway, Central ☎ 2868 3993 🕐 Daily 10–7
🚇 Admiralty

LI YUEN STREET MARKET
A clothes, handbag, fabric and accessories market, one of Hong Kong's oldest, with some excellent bargains, particularly in leather goods. It could be combined with the factory outlets in the Pedder Building.
➕ C10 ✉ Off Queen's Road Central, Central 🕐 Daily 12–late 🚇 Central

MARBLE ROAD MARKET
This busy working local market sells fresh produce and there are bargains in T-shirts and clothes. A fish market is nearby.
➕ Off map ✉ Marble Road, North Point 🕐 Daily 12–late
🚋 Tram from Causeway Bay, Wan Chai or Central

MOUNTAIN FOLKCRAFT
Delightful handmade paintings, carvings and *batik* from Southeast Asia.
➕ C10 ✉ 12 Wo On Lane, Central ☎ 2523 2817
🕐 Mon–Sat 9.30–6.30
🚇 Central

PACIFIC PLACE
A collection of designer outlets and local chain stores. This mall has an

Alfred Dunhill, Ermenegildo Zegna, Hugo, Swank Shop, plus a Marks & Spencer, Lane Crawford and several local retailers selling casual separates at basic prices.
➕ E10 ✉ 1 Pacific Place, 88 Queensway ☎ 2844 8900
🕐 Daily 10–8 🚇 Admiralty

PEDDER BUILDING
Five floors of tiny shops, all with something worth poking around for. Not all are factory outlets, and some sell both regular designer goods and discounted items, so browse carefully.
➕ D10 ✉ 12 Pedder Street, Central 🚇 Central

UPPER LASCAR ROW (CAT STREET)
A flea market set alongside more expensive shops and selling the same kind of bric-a-brac, records and curios, along with the occasional antique.
➕ B9 ✉ Off Queen's Road West, Sheung Wan 🕐 Daily 11–6 🚇 Sheung Wan

VINCENT SUM DESIGNS
A handicraft shop that stocks lots of interesting and pretty *batik* cloth as well as clothes made from ethnic prints.
➕ C10 ✉ 15 Lyndhurst Terrace, Central ☎ 2542 2610
🕐 Daily 10–6 🚇 Central

Entertainment and Nightlife

CARNEGIE'S

An interesting nightspot where the music shifts genre regularly but is often from local bands. It's loud and there's usually a crush on the dance floor.

🔒 F10 ✉ 53 Lockhart Road, Wan Chai ☎ 2866 6289 🕐 Mon-Sat 11am-3am, Sun 5pm-2am 🚇 Wan Chai

CLUB ING

Draws hip young Hong Kong girls; this place tries to bill itself as très chic, but many say it's missing the mark. Still it's packed every weekend.

🔒 F10 ✉ 4th floor, New World Harbour View Hotel, 1 Harbour Road, Wan Chai ☎ 2824 0523 🕐 Mon-Sat 5pm-4am 🚇 Wan Chai

COCONUTS

Cool and unpretentious with a tropical theme, this laid-back bar entices locals and tourists alike with coconut cocktails, pizzas and chilled-out house music. The plasma screens and mood lighting combine with the street-side tables and palm trees to give a relaxing Caribbean feel.

🔒 C10 ✉ Ground floor, 5 Lan Kwai Fong, Central ☎ 2801 6862 🕐 Sun-Thu noon-1am; Fri-Sat noon-3am 🚇 Central

DICKENS BAR

A Dickensian place that's one of Hong Kong's best bars. Bands change constantly—Irish, West Indian, Indonesian and Filipino—and there's jazz Sunday afternoons.

🔒 G10 ✉ Lower Ground Floor, Excelsior Hotel, 281 Gloucester Road, Causeway Bay ☎ 2837 6782 🕐 Sun-Thu 11am-1am, Fri-Sat 11am-2am 🚇 Causeway Bay

LA DOLCE VITA

Popular with office workers in the early evening, but a great place for people-watching by night.

🔒 C10 ✉ Cosmos Building, 9-11 Lan Kwai Fong ☎ 2186 1888 🕐 Mon-Thu 11.30am-2am, Fri 12.30-3am, Sat 12.30-3am, Sun 4pm-1am 🚇 Central

DRAGON-I

The coolest bar in Hong Kong where all the really hip people go. Bar, restaurant and a terrace

---

---

overlooking Wyndham Street. Lots of dancing too. Happy hours 6pm-9pm.

🔒 C10 ✉ Upper ground floor, The Centrium, 60 Wyndham Street, Central ☎ 3110 1222 🕐 Mon-Sat noon-midnight 🚇 Central

DROP

This is a seriously cool place to be and comes highly recommended by locals and visitors alike. It's very small and so has a members-only restriction on weekends, which is loosely enforced. Early evening it's a cocktail lounge, serving fresh fruit cocktails. DJs later.

🔒 C10 ✉ On Lok Mansion, 39-43 Hollywood Road, Central ☎ 2543 8856 🕐 Tue 7pm-2am, Wed 7pm-4 am, Thu 7pm-5am, Fri 10pm-5am, Sat-Sun 8pm-4am 🚇 Central

THE DUBLIN JACK

Packed with regulars on weekends, this friendly place fills to overflowing toward the end of the week, as it's *the* established pub for Central office workers.

🔒 C10 ✉ 37-43 Cochrane Street (next to escalator), Central ☎ 2543 0081 🕐 Daily 11am-12.30am 🚇 Central

FOUR SEASONS SPA

With private spa treatment rooms available, and a wide choice of therapies, you could easily pass away a day

enjoying facilities such as a vitality pool, flotation tank or aromatherapy massage. Perfect for easing the stresses and strains of the day.
🔒 C9 ✉ 8 Finance Street, Central ☎ 3196 8888 🕐 8am–10pm 🚇 Central

FRINGE CLUB
The main venue for non-mainstream performance art, as well as interesting drama workshops. During the Arts Festival alternative offerings are usually staged here. Often the themes are local and showcase amateur actors.
🔒 C10 ✉ 2 Lower Albert Road, Central ☎ 2521 7251 🕐 Mon–Thu noon–midnight, Fri, Sat noon–3am 🚇 Central

GOETHE INSTITUTE
The German Cultural Institute regularly organizes films, exhibitions and events about German culture and language in the Hong Kong Arts Centre.
🔒 E10 ✉ 14th floor, Hong Kong Arts Centre, 2 Harbour Road, Wan Chai ☎ 2802 0088 🚇 Wan Chai

HARDY'S FOLK CLUB
Not as folksy as its name suggests but still a viable alternative to the heavy metal, rock and jazz venues. Come just for a drink, or have a meal.
🔒 C10 ✉ 35 D'Aguilar Street, Central ☎ 2522 4448 🕐 Daily 5.30pm–2am 🚇 Central

HONG KONG ACADEMY FOR PERFORMING ARTS
www.hkapa.edu
This arts school next to the Arts Centre has different-size theaters, plus an outdoor venue. It concentrates on classical dance, drama and music.
🔒 E10 ✉ 1 Gloucester Road, Wan Chai ☎ 2584 8500 🚇 Wan Chai

HONG KONG ARTS CENTRE
www.hkac.org.hk
Drama and music of diverse kinds take place here.
🔒 F10 ✉ 2 Harbour Road, Wan Chai ☎ 2582 0200 🚇 Wan Chai

HONG KONG CITY HALL
www.lcd.gov.hk/ce/cultural service/cityhall
The stage, auditorium and recital hall here host a wide variety of local and visiting artists.

ISLAND NIGHTLIFE

Lan Kwai Fong, in Central, is where the see-and-be-seen crowd spends their money on over-priced drinks. Wan Chai, once seedy, is now one of the hippest nightlife areas in town. Soho (south of Hollywood Road) is a popular dining and drinking area for expats. Stanley is unique—more relaxed and meditative than other areas.

🔒 D10 ✉ 7 Edinburgh Place, Central ☎ 2734 9009 🚇 Central

INSOMNIA
This place has been around long enough to have collected a loyal clientele. It has two bars and live music after 10.30pm. Happy hours 5–9. The place fills up in the early hours and especially so on weekends. All day (and night) menu of simple dishes.
🔒 C10 ✉ Ho Lee Commercial Building, 34–44 D'Aguilar Street, Central ☎ 2525 0957 🕐 Mon–Sat 9am–6am, Sun 2pm–5am 🚇 Central

JOE BANANAS
Very trendy American-style bar, disco and restaurant. Long hours at weekends; men must wear a shirt with collar.
🔒 F11 ✉ 23 Luard Road, Wan Chai ☎ 2529 1811 🕐 Daily Mon–Thu 11am–5am, Fri, Sat 11am–6am, Sun and holidays noon–4am 🚇 Wan Chai

STAUNTON'S WINE BAR & CAFÉ
Packed to the gills most nights, this bar by the Soho escalators remains one of the most popular in town.
🔒 C10 ✉ 16A Staunton Street ☎ 2869 7652 🕐 Daily 9am–midnight 🚇 Central

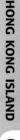
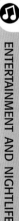

Restaurants

PRICES

Prices are approximate, based on a 3-course meal for one person.

$$$	over HK$700
$$	HK$300–HK$700
$	under HK$300

AL'S DINER ($$)

First-rate sirloin from the US goes into the fair-sized burgers. There's lots of 1950s chrome and neon, and a juke box churns out period songs.
🚹 C10 ✉ Room F, Ground floor, Winner Building, 27–37 D'Aguilar Street, Central ☎ 2869 1869 🕐 Mon–Thu 11am–12.30am, Fri, Sat 11am–3am, Sun 12pm–12.30am 🚇 Central

AMIGO RESTAURANT ($$$)

Spanish setting, French fare (*filet de sole Marquis, crevettes au gruyère*). Set meals are less expensive and less formal at lunchtime.
🚹 G11 ✉ Amigo Mansion, 79A Wong Nei Chung Road, Happy Valley ☎ 2577 2202 🕐 Daily 12–3, 6–midnight 🚋 Tram from Central

THE ASHOKA RESTAURANT ($)

Delicious curries, tandoori and vegetarian dishes and other spicy fare. Clean and comfortable.
🚹 C10 ✉ Ground floor, 57 Wyndham Street, Central ☎ 2524 9623 🕐 Daily 12–2.30, 6–11.30 🚇 Central

BOCA ($$)

For a tapas and good wine—at a reasonable price—check out this popular Soho restaurant/bar.
🚹 C10 ✉ 65 Peel Street, Central ☎ 2548 1717 🕐 Daily 12–11 🚇 Central

BRASSERIE LE FAUCHON ($$)

The prices here are lower than other French restaurants around the territory but the quality remains high. The food is prepared by expertly trained local chefs using imported French ingredients and tastes fantastic. The interior is cool and light. All round a highly enjoyable meal can be had here.
🚹 C10 ✉ Ground floor, 45 Elgin Street, Central ☎ 2526 8318 🕐 Daily 11.30–2.30, 6.30–11 🚇 Central

DIM SUM

The most traditional of Cantonese meals, dim sum (literally "small heart") is served from early morning to late afternoon in Cantonese restaurants all over the city. The dishes arrive in bamboo baskets piled high on a tray or trolley. As the servers circulate with the trolleys, just point at whatever takes your fancy. Popular dumplings include *har gau* (shrimps), *pai kwat* (spareribs) and *woo kok* (vegetarian). You pay according to how many dishes you consume.

BRASSERIE ON THE EIGHTH ($$$)

Superb French fare—in small portions—with excellent service and lovely views.
🚹 E11 ✉ 8th floor, Conrad International Hotel, Pacific Place, Admiralty ☎ 2521 3838, Ext. 8270 🕐 Daily 12–3, 6–11 🚇 Admiralty

CAMMINO ($$)

Bringing a little taste of Italy to the heart of Causeway Bay, this restaurant works overtime at making you feel you are somewhere else. Great Italian food from the various regions of Italy in an intimate, quiet environment.
🚹 G10 ✉ The Excelsior Hotel, 281 Gloucester Road, Causeway Bay ☎ 2837 6780 🕐 Mon–Sat 12–2.30pm, daily 6–11 🚇 Causeway Bay

CAPRICE ($$$)

Lavish and exquisite, this restaurant carries the prestige and allure of Vincent Thierry, chef of Le Cinq in Paris. If your plastic can take the strain and you're lucky enough to have a reservation then you will enjoy food and service of the highest quality, along with a magnificent art nouveau styled setting and great harbor views.
🚹 D9 ✉ 8 Finance Street, Central ☎ 3196 8888 🕐 Daily 12–2.30, Mon–Sun 6–10.30 🚇 Central

!CARAMBA ($$)

Spicy Mexican food with Chinese overtones is served up with plenty of tequila at this spot in chic Soho. Try the scrumptious tortilla chips. Reserve ahead for weekends.

C10 ⊠ 26–30 Elgin Street, Central ☎ 2530 9963 ⊙ Daily noon–midnight ⊜ Central

CHEF ($$)

Stylish and contemporary Japanese restaurant serving traditional sushi, sashimi and fusion cuisine. Hosts live teppan-yaki performances.

C10 ⊠ 20–22 D'Aguilar Street, Central ☎ 2525 6628 ⊙ Daily 11am–1am ⊜ Central

LA COMIDA ($$)

With bright yellow walls, hanging plates and a traditional feel, this authentic Spanish eatery comes recommended by local office workers. The menu includes an array of tapas and paellas.

C10 ⊠ Ground floor, 22 Staunton Street ☎ 2530 3118 ⊙ Daily 12–2.30pm, Sun–Thu 6–10.30, Fri, Sat 6–11 ⊜ Central

COYOTE ($$)

Slurp down one of the 56 varieties of margaritas, and to soak it up launch into a monstrous plate of *nachos simpaticos*.

F10 ⊠ 114–120 Lockhart Road, Wan Chai ☎ 2861 2221 ⊙ Daily 11.30am–midnight ⊜ Fortress Hill

THE CURRY POT ($)

Curries from across Southeast Asia and the Indian subcontinent to tantalize the tastebuds of both vegetarians and meat-eaters.

F10 ⊠ 68–70 Lockhart Road, Wan Chai ☎ 2865 6099 ⊙ Daily 6am–11pm ⊜ Wan Chai

HANG FOOK LAU ($–$$)

A loud, bright, busy place to enjoy authentic Cantonese food at down-to-earth prices. Popular with locals for lunch. Seafood hotpot is very good and varies every day according to what is available.

F10 ⊠ 1st floor, Hay Wah Mansion, 71–85 Hennessy Road, Wan Chai ☎ 2528 2468 ⊙ 7am–midnight ⊜ Wan Chai

---

INDOCHINE 129 ($$)

The French influence on Vietnamese food is very apparent in the menu of this restaurant, with its colonial-style setting. Good place to try out Vietnamese food for the first time.

C10 ⊠ 2nd floor, California Tower, 30–32 D'Aguilar Street, Central ☎ 2869 7399 ⊙ Mon–Sat 12–2.30pm, daily 6.30–11 ⊜ Central

JIMMY'S KITCHEN ($$)

Its history stretches back to the 1920s, venerable for Hong Kong, and its menu can be relied on for its signature goulash, borscht and stroganoff. Comfortable and traditional with equally reliable service.

C10 ⊠ Basement, South China Building, 1 Wyndham Street, Central ☎ 2526 5293 ⊙ Daily noon–midnight ⊜ Central

JUMBO FLOATING RESTAURANT ($$$)

Alone, this highly decorated boat is a tourist attraction in itself. A night out that begins with a free ferry ride in a small sampan across the harbor. Dim sum 7am to 5pm.

Farther afield map ⊠ Shun Wan, Wong Chuk Hang, Aberdeen ☎ 2553 9111 ⊙ Daily 1am–11pm ⊟ 7, 70 from Central Bus Terminal

LOBSTER BAR AND GRILL ($$$)

Swanky, relaxed place with live bands to serenade you. Innovative modern European menu—try bluefin tuna with asparagus and eggplant (aubergine) salad or the seared chicken breast with scallops and fennel. Nice bar, too.

⊞ E11 ✉ Island Shangri-La, Pacific Place, Supreme Court Road, Central ☎ 2820 8560 ⊙ Daily 12–2.30pm, 6.30–10 ⊒ Central

MAN WAH RESTAURANT ($$$)

Unlike most Chinese restaurants, the Man Wah is dimly lit, intimate and elegant, as you would expect in one of Hong Kong's best hotels. The food is excellent and worth the money.

⊞ D10 ✉ Mandarin Oriental Hotel, 5 Connaught Road, Central ☎ 2522 0111 ⊙ Daily 7am–11am, Mon–Fri 12–3, 6.30–11 ⊒ Central

PEAK CAFÉ ($)

This bar and café cannot be missed from the Mid Levels escalator route in the center of Soho. Inside is a unique mixture of old world Chinese decor, Gothic stonework and chandeliers.

⊞ C10 ✉ 9–13 Shelley Street, Central ☎ 2140 6877 ⊙ Mon–Fri 11am–2am, Sat 9am–2am, Sun 9am–midnight ⊒ Central

TANDOOR RESTAURANT ($$–$$$)

A classy restaurant with rosewood furniture, lunch and dinner buffets and a wide-ranging menu. Try the betelnut-based desserts.

⊞ C10 ✉ 1st floor, Lyndhurst Tower, 1 Lyndhurst Terrace, Central ☎ 2845 2262 ⊙ Daily 12–2.30pm, 6–10.45 ⊒ Central

LE TIRE BOUCHON ($$–$$$)

Tucked away down Graham Street, downhill from the main Soho run of Staunton Street, this top-notch restaurant lays claim to being Hong Kong's original French restaurant. The food is authentic and intense; the interior is classic and cozy. Connoisseurs will also value the extensive

wine list of more than 180 bottles from around the world.

⊞ C10 ✉ 45 Graham Street, Central ☎ 2523 5459 ⊙ Mon–Sat 12–2.30pm, 6.30–10.30 ⊒ Central

TOKIO JOE ($$)

Very trendy spot in Lan Kwai Fong serving excellent sushi and sashimi, as well as filled rolls and hot dishes. The same company has two more Japanese places in the area, Kyoto Joe and Joe's Yaki, which are more like teppanyaki bars.

⊞ C10 ✉ 16 Lan Kwai Fong, Central ☎ 2525 1889 ⊙ Mon–Sat 12–2.30, 6.30–11, Sun 6.30–11 ⊒ Central

YUNG KEE RESTAURANT ($$–$$$)

This long-standing favorite among local people is put forward as *the* number one place to eat Cantonese cuisine in the area. Yung Kee has a list of prestigious awards to support this belief. The restaurant is highly visible in the heart of the Central district, with a large glamorous shop front and valet parking.

⊞ C10 ✉ 32–40 Wellington Street, Central ☎ 2522 1624 ⊙ 11–11 ⊒ Central

Less glamorous than its neighbor over the water, densely populated Kowloon is where the real daily life of Hong Kong happens. Shops are thick on the ground and if you have a hankering for real Chinese food this is where you'll find it.

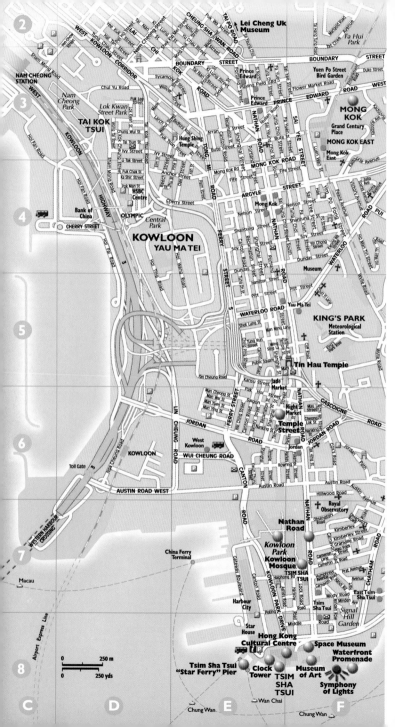

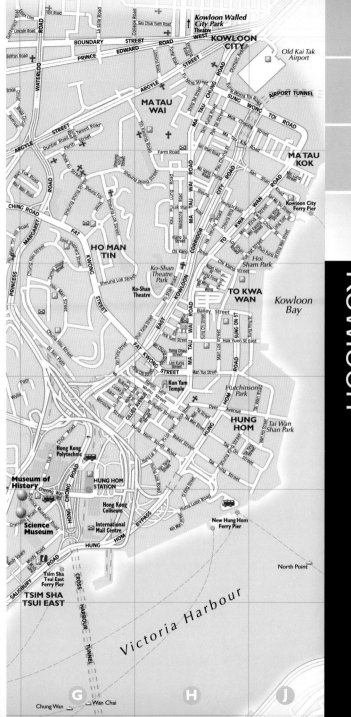

Kowloon Walled City Park

This park stands on the site of the former Walled City

THE BASICS

Off map at H2
Junction of Tung Tau Tsuen and Tung Tsing roads, Kowloon
Daily 6.30am–11pm
Lok Fu
Good
Free

HIGHLIGHTS

● Pretty, quiet space in the middle of Kowloon
● Turtle and goldfish ponds
● Artistic topiary
● Renovated administrative building

TIPS

● This is a great place to bring a picnic.
● If you have your own chess pieces, you can have a game on the park's large Chinese chessboards.

Once the most notorious, lawless and poverty stricken place in Hong Kong, Kowloon Walled City is now a manicured park, filled with pavilions, topiary and shady walks. Even the shrubs have been cut and shaped into animal figures.

From ruin to park In 1898 when Britain leased the New Territories from China, Kowloon Walled City was a Chinese garrison and was never included in any agreement. The two countries bickered over its jurisdiction for almost 100 years while the place became ever more ramshackle, with blocks of tenements raised without any kind of planning, nonexistent sanitation and frequent outbreaks of disease. During World War II the Japanese knocked the actual walls down to extend the old Kai Tak airport and thousands of illegal immigrants from China found a post-war refuge there. The two governments finally reached a settlement over the area in 1987, the 30,000 inhabitants were rehoused and the buildings were flattened, archaeologists rummaged around and finally a park was built in the ruins. The park is complete with pagodas, a Chinese zodiac garden, a mountain view pavilion and a hilltop pavilion.

Historic survivor One of the original buildings of the fort, the Yamen, dating back to the 19th century, has been restored and now holds a display of photos and other items concerning the history of the Walled City. Also discovered in the clearance were the stone plaques that marked the south gate of the Walled City.

Modern art on display (below) at the Museum of Art (below right)

Museum of Art

A beautifully laid-out series of galleries contains displays of exquisite Chinese calligraphy and painting, both traditional and modern, many stunning ancient artifacts and a collection of jade, ivory and pottery.

Chinese antiquities The museum has seven galleries; four contain Chinese antiquities, local artists' work and pictures that are of historical note as well as artistic worth. The thousands of exhibits in the Chinese antiquities section range from rhino-horn cups to burial goods and lavish tomb adornments; of particular interest are two large Tang dynasty (AD618–906) tomb guardians in the form of mythical beasts. The jade and ivory carvings in the decorative arts gallery are especially lovely.

Art galleries The best gallery is the one containing old pictures and prints of Hong Kong. It is hard to believe that the sandy beaches and jungle-filled hills could have become such a different kind of jungle in so short a space of time. It is a revelation of just how far the colony has come since the early 19th century.

Modern art The works in the contemporary art gallery are divided into decades, and it is particularly interesting to see the development of local art since the 1950s. There is also a collection of calligraphy and Chinese paintings, and a special gallery for international exhibitions. Between galleries, leather armchairs facing the enormous corridor windows allow you to enjoy the waterfront vista.

THE BASICS

www.lcsd/gov.hk/CE/Museum/Arts

➕ F8

✉ 10 Salisbury Road (next door to Hong Kong Cultural Centre)

☎ 2721 0116

🕐 Fri–Wed 10–6. Closed some public holidays

🍴 Museum café

Ⓜ Tsim Sha Tsui

🚌 Tsim Sha Tsui bus station

⛴ Star Ferry from Wan Chai and Central to Tsim Sha Tsui

♿ Excellent

✋ Inexpensive

❓ Museum bookshop

HIGHLIGHTS

● Han-dynasty pottery watchtower
● Tang-dynasty tomb guardians
● Translucent rhino-horn cups
● Painting of Wyndham Street
● Model of Guangzhou

KOWLOON ★ **TOP 25**

Museum of History

This museum covers thousands of years of Hong Kong's history

This gem of a museum, both user-friendly and informative, is a good place to spend an hour or two, especially as the curators frequently introduce new touring shows and exhibits.

Prehistory to the handover When the administrative body of HK SAR built this new $390 million history museum you had to wonder at how they might choose to rearrange the history of the island now the Brits had left. But have no fear—the museum is an excellent portrayal of the area from prehistory to the handover. The displays are interactive, with sounds and smells, and there are even walk-through exhibits like a Hakka family dwelling or an early tram.

Exhibits The natural history section documents most of the wildlife that has ever roamed these parts, while the archaeology area, covering about 6,000 years of history, tells the story of the island's earliest settlers. Most of the objects uncovered at Lei Cheng Uk (▷ 67) are here, too. There's an ethnography section explaining where all the Hong Kongers originated from (but not much on more recent immigrants). The real interest of the museum though, is its account of more recent history. There are exhibits on the Japanese occupation (laid out as an air-raid shelter), Hong Kong's recent development and even a bit about what has happened since it became one of China's SARs. Stamps, old documents and a huge photographic collection make a visit to this fascinating museum anything but dull.

THE BASICS

http://hk.history.museum

✚ F7

✉ 100 Chatham Road South, Tsim Sha Tsui

☎ 2724 9042

🕐 Mon, Wed–Sat 10–6, Sun 10–7

🍴 Café in museum (closed Tue)

🚇 Tsim Sha Tsui

🚌 5, 5C, 8 from Star Ferry

♿ Excellent

💵 Inexpensive (free Wed)

❓ Guided tours in English twice daily on Sat, Sun

HIGHLIGHTS

● The photographic collection
● Reconstructions of a tea shop, grocer's, barber's and cinema from the 1960s
● The re-created street from the early years of the last century with tram, boat, herbalists and more
● Reconstruction of the Bogue forts used in the Opium Wars

Interactive exhibits at the Science Museum, including Hong Kong's first airliner (below)

The Science Museum is one of Hong Kong's most popular attractions. In such a modern city, some the 500 major exhibits feel a bit old-fashioned these days, but children will still love them.

Still popular Exhibitions include objects from the past as well as explaining how everyday items function, and some focus on the science and technology particularly relevant to Hong Kong. The museum's 18 galleries on four floors contain thousands of exhibits, most of them interactive, especially in the children's areas. Topics cover all aspects of science but it's the sheer scale of some of the exhibits that makes the science interesting. In one gallery a DC3 plane hangs from the ceiling, while a kinetic Energy Machine rises through all four floors of the museum and sees hundreds of balls sent pulsing around a metallic labyrinth.

For children The museum is definitely a child-oriented place and on weekdays hordes of them come here in school parties, although perhaps that's half the fun of it. Two exhibits are particularly in demand here—an entire car linked up to a video screen where children can try to drive around the computer-simulated road in front of them and a similar setup with an entire light air-craft. Exhibits cover the entire spectrum of science-related subjects, from electricity and magnetism to a breakdown of what you eat. There are robot arms to operate, buttons to push and a very scary machine that calculates the minute-by-minute increase in the world's population.

THE BASICS

http://hk.science.museum
G7
2 Science Museum Road, Tsim Sha Tsui East
2732 3232
Mon–Wed, Fri 1–9, Sat– Sun 10–9
Café
Jordan, Tsim Sha Tsui
5, 5C, 8 from Star Ferry
Good
Moderate (free Wed)

HIGHLIGHTS

● Simulated interactive rides
● Giant Energy Tower
● Irresistible knobs to press
● Watching the school parties swarm onto the exhibits

TIPS

● School parties usually arrive mid-afternoon.
● Sunday is a very popular day for families.
● The Museum of History is right across the road if you want to make a day of it.

Space Museum

HIGHLIGHTS

● Omnimax shows
● *Mercury* space capsule
● Hall of Space Science
● Solar telescope
● Planetarium show
● Hall of Astronomy

TIPS

● Some of the interactive exhibits have height and weight restrictions.
● If there is a typhoon or a black rainstorm warning, the museum will close.

This museum, which has one of the world's largest and most advanced planetariums, is fascinating for kids, with plenty of hands-on exhibits, a *Mercury* space capsule and daily Space Theatre shows.

Layout and Omnimax The museum's oval, pink building, built in 1980 by the Architectural Services Department, is in itself stunning. Inside are three exhibitions: the Hall of Astronomy, the Hall of Space Science and, the most popular, the Stanley Ho Space Theatre with its 75ft (23m) screen. If you haven't seen an Omnimax film before, then seize the chance here. You sit back in tilted seats and gaze ahead and up at a screen that covers most of the ceiling and front wall. The shows here alternate between star shows using a star projector and Omnimax shows from around the

A solar system display in the Hall of Astonomy (below left); a replica of a protective suit used by Apollo astronauts on the moon landing (below middle) and a model of Space Shuttle Columbia *in the Hall of Space Science (below right)*

world. The size of the screen allows an almost 360-degree panorama.

Exhibition halls The Hall of Space Science includes bits of moon rock, the actual *Mercury* space capsule piloted by Scott Carpenter in 1962, and lots of information about China's current space program. In the Hall of Astronomy there is a solar telescope where you can look directly at the sun. Did you know that it was ancient Chinese astronomers who were the first to spot Halley's Comet and the first to chart the movements of the stars? The interactive simulators include a gyroscope and models allowing you to launch spaceships, land a craft on the moon, take a moon walk or go hang gliding. This is a grand place for visitors with children and those interested in space. Outside is a statue garden.

THE BASICS

✚ F8

✉ 10 Salisbury Road (next to Hong Kong Cultural Centre), Tsim Sha Tsui

☎ 2721 0226

🕐 Sat–Sun 10–9, Mon, Wed–Fri 1–9

🚇 Tsim Sha Tsui

🚌 Tsim Sha Tsui bus station

⛴ Star Ferry from Central and Wan Chai to Tsim Sha Tsui

♿ Excellent

💷 Inexpensive

❓ Children under 3 are not allowed in Omnimax

HIGHLIGHTS

- Shops in Tsim Sha Tsui ferry terminal
- Vista to east and west along shipping lane
- Hong Kong & Shanghai Banking Corporation Building
- Bank of China Tower
- Convention and Exhibition Centre
- Views of Peak and Mid Levels

The Star Ferry journey has to be one of the world's most spectacular sea crossings. You get a panoramic view of the harbor as you ply around dredgers, launches and all the other vessels.

Looking back The journey time on the Star Ferry, which has been operating between Kowloon and Hong Kong Island since 1898, is less than 10 minutes on a good day, but the views of the cityscape on both sides of the harbor are excellent—and all for HK$2.20 (less for the lower deck). The ferry terminal on the Tsim Sha Tsui side sits beside the incongruous Hong Kong Cultural Centre (1989), with its windowless, smooth-tiled surface (▷ 67). As the ferry sets off to Hong Kong Island, you can see the long pink-and-black striped outlines of the Museum of Art (▷ 55).

Riding the Star Ferry across Victoria Harbour is something every visitor to Hong Kong should experience

CENTRAL & WAN
中區及灣仔

Looking forward Ahead, on the island itself, the stunning architecture of the reclaimed shoreline spikes the sky, dominated by the Convention and Exhibition Centre, which opened in 1988, with its twin towers of New World Harbour View and Hyatt hotels. It was built in two phases, the first by architects Mr. Ng Chun & Associates, the second by Wong & Ouyang. Behind it is Central Plaza (▷ 28) and the IFC Buildings. West of these buildings are the General Post Office and the striped towers of the Stock Exchange, built by Remo Riva in 1986. Behind these are the Hong Kong & Shanghai Banking Corporation Building (▷ 41), all glass and innards, and Pei's controversial Bank of China Tower (▷ 40). In 2006 the old Edinburgh Place ferry terminal was replaced by new piers in front of the IFC 2 tower. The walk to the commercial area is longer from here.

THE BASICS

www.starferry.com.hk
☐ E8
✉ Salisbury Road, Tsim Sha Tsui (Kowloon); Mon Yui Street, Central (Hong Kong Island); Sea Front Road, Wan Chai (Hong Kong Island)
☎ Hotline: 2367 7065
🕑 Daily 6.30am–11.30pm. Office: 8.30am–6.30pm
🍴 Cafés, bakeries at Central ferry terminal gate
🚇 Tsim Sha Tsui (Kowloon); Central, Wan Chai (Hong Kong Island)
♿ Lower decks more accessible
💲 Inexpensive

Symphony of Lights

HIGHLIGHTS

● Harbor trip
● The cool of the Tsim Sha Tsui promenade
● Occasional pyrotechnic additions to the show
● The view beyond the harborfront to the Peak

TIPS

● Several tour companies offer 1.5-hour, drinks-included tours of the harbor.
● Star Ferries' tour (no drinks) is the least expensive at HK$140 for 2 hours.

Victoria Harbour has to be one of the most amazing sights of a trip to Hong Kong. Each evening a stunning sound-and-light show takes place creating a vibrant frenzy along the waterfront.

Dazzling display Impressive though it has always been, Victoria Harbour is even more striking since the introduction of a Symphony of Lights. It is a stirring experience to stand and watch this 18-minute performance by the buildings along the waterfront on Hong Kong Island and Kowloon. Every day at 8pm the exteriors of 44 of the city's major buildings glow with a myriad of vivid colors with the use of a wide range of architectural lights to draw the eye along the waterfront. Best viewed from Tsim Sha Tsui, the spectacle sees one building after another light up, highlighting its outline or

Spectacular views of the skyscrapers on Hong Kong Island are lit up by the dazzling Symphony of Lights

changing its appearance altogether. With the addition of several buildings Kowloon-side, the lights and lasers reach across the harbor turning the whole area into a dazzling display. A narration and music are broadcast each night (in English on Monday, Wednesday and Friday) along the Avenue of Stars, while onlookers from Tsim Sha Tsui and Golden Bauhinia Square in Wan Chai can tune into the narration by radio (English channel available on 103.4FM). On certain special occasions the light display is complemented by rooftop pyrotechnic displays on some buildings. You can also take one of the harbor cruises and listen to the narration and music piped aboard.

Take an evening stroll The display is recognized by the Guinness Book of Records as the largest permanent sound-and-light show in the world.

THE BASICS

www.tourism.gov.hk
/symphony

⊞ F8

🕐 8pm–8.18pm

🚇 Tsim Sha Tsui, Wan Chai

♿ Good

✋ Free

Temple Street

Grab a bargain at Temple Street Night Market

THE BASICS

➕ E6
✉ Temple Street, Kansu Street, Reclamation Street, Kowloon
🕐 Jade market: 10–5. Temple Street market: 4pm–midnight. Vegetable market: early morning and early evening
🍴 Seafood restaurants and hawker area on Temple Street
🚇 Jordan
♿ Good
💵 Free

HIGHLIGHTS

● Fresh fish for sale
● Fortune-tellers
● Chinese medicine shops
● Shops selling traditional Chinese wedding clothes
● Jade market
● Yau Ma Tei Typhoon Shelter, to the west
● Racks of T-shirts
● Exotic vegetables in vegetable market

At about 7pm each night, stands sprout on either side of this street and are hung with T-shirts, lingerie, jeans and other goodies. Earlier in the day, nearby stalls do a brisk trade in jade.

After dark The market is full of bargains in silk shirts, leather items, jeans and T-shirts. Nothing on sale is really indigenous as locals rather than the visitors are the buyers. After about 7.30pm the street is closed to traffic, and at the crossroads in the middle of the market, two fish restaurants set up their tables. Their counters, out in the street, contain all manner of wriggling things that you can pick out to be cooked for your dinner.

Jade for sale Close by, near the junction of Battery and Kansu streets under an overpass, is the jade market. Here, until they close up at about 5pm, hundreds of stands sell all kinds of jade, which comes in many shades besides green—from white through to purple. Locals spend the afternoon bargaining over prices, which range from inexpensive to a king's ransom.

Still more In adjoining streets are vegetable and fruit sellers, shops selling fabrics and traditional red-embroidered Chinese wedding outfits and many Chinese medicine shops. If you are lucky, you may catch a Chinese opera performance, sung in Cantonese, on a makeshift stage of bamboo and canvas. As you walk through the market, look for people playing the age-old game of mahjong in the backs of shops or set up in corners.

TOP 25 **Waterfront Promenade**

The views of Hong Kong Island and the harbor are outstanding all along the length of this promenade on the Kowloon waterfront.

Avenue of Stars Even before the creation of the Avenue of Stars the Waterfront Promenade was an excellent place for an evening's stroll, close to the chaos of Nathan Road but serene, and above all, relatively unpopulated, especially toward its eastern end popular with old fishermen and canoodling lovers. Nowadays the 0.25-mile (400m) Avenue of Stars, a tribute to the 100 years or so of movie making in Hong Kong, draws the crowds. Represented here are some of the people responsible for the enormous success of the industry. Lots of the stars have sunk their handprints into the cement blocks set into the ground, while there are a few others yet to turn up and oblige.

Statues There are also statues of the stars and a giant model of the statuette given out at the Hong Kong Awards ceremony each year. All the big names are here plus some you may never have heard of. Accompanying the plaques is a series of pillars that tell the history of film making. The life-like statue of Bruce Lee was built from funds donated by his fans.

Weekends On weekends you will see wedding couples posing by the statues with the skyline of Hong Kong Island behind them. On Saturday evenings there are free music performances.

THE BASICS

- F8
- ⊠ Salisbury Road
- ¶¶ Nearby
- ⬚ Tsim Sha Tsui
- ⬚ Excellent
- ⬚ Free

HIGHLIGHTS

- Statue of Jackie Chan
- The view of the harbor
- Watching people posing by the statues
- The quieter eastern end

TIPS

- The evening is the best time to visit when the cement hand impressions give way to the skyline.
- The Avenue is a good place to watch the Symphony of Lights.

KOWLOON

★

TOP 25

CLOCK TOWER

The 148ft (45m) clock tower is all that remains of the Kowloon–Canton Railway Station, which was demolished in 1978 to make room for the Cultural Centre (▷ below).

➕ E8 ✉ Salisbury Road 🍴 Nearby
🚇 Tsim Sha Tsui ♿ Excellent

HONG KONG CULTURAL CENTRE

Designed by the government's architectural services department in 1989, this is one of Hong Kong's most controversial buildings. It has a huge sloping roof that is matched by the dome of the nearby Space Museum, and is uniformly pink. The building is also windowless—rather odd as it would have one of the most dynamic views in the world. Inside, it is all very modern, especially the sparse auditoria with their apparently unsupported balconies. At the rear is a waterfront walkway.

➕ E/F8 ✉ Salisbury Road, Tsim Sha Tsui
☎ 3185 1612 🚇 Tsim Sha Tsui
✋ Free

KOWLOON MOSQUE

The present mosque was built in 1984 on the site of an earlier 19th-century one. It is the largest mosque in the city, catering to thousands of Muslims.

➕ F7 ✉ Corner of Nathan and Haiphong roads ☎ 2724 0095 to arrange a visit
🕐 Closed to general public 🍴 Nearby
🚇 Tsim Sha Tsui

KOWLOON PARK

One of the most engaging green spaces in the city, Kowloon Park is full of good things to do. There's an open-air swimming pool, a heated indoor pool, an aviary, a Chinese garden, a maze and a sculpture garden. In the morning you can watch people practising t'ai chi.

➕ E7 ✉ Nathan Road 🕐 Daily 5am–midnight 🍴 Cafés and restaurants in Nathan Road 🚇 Tsim Sha Tsui ♿ Poor
✋ Free

LEI CHENG UK TOMB MUSEUM

Although built over an ancient Han dynasty tomb, this little museum is

Kowloon Mosque (above)

The Clock Tower (left)

Lei Cheng Uk Museum (right)

now surrounded by high-rise apartments occupied by thousands of Hong Kong people. This continuity between the living and the dead, spanning 2,000 years, is very moving.

➕ Off map at D1 ✉ 41 Tonkin Street, Sham Shui Po ☎ 2386 2863 🕐 Mon–Wed, Fri, Sat 10–6, Sun 1–6. Closed 25–26 Dec and first 3 days of Chinese New Year 🚇 Cheung Sha Wan 🚌 2 from Star Ferry to Po On Road ♿ Good access to museum displays but not to tomb 🎟 Free

MONG KOK

Although not on the main tourist route, Mong Kok's crowded streets, tenements and markets are well worth experiencing. The most popular markets include the Bird Garden, the Ladies Market, the Flower Market and the Goldfish Market.

➕ F3 🚇 Mong Kok MTR, KCR ♿ Poor

NATHAN ROAD

Formerly called Robinson Road, it acquired its present name from Sir Matthew Nathan, a governor of Hong Kong in the early 20th century. The road is 3.2 miles (5km) long; the southern stretch is known as the "Golden Mile", due to the high price of real estate and the large numbers of shops and businesses.

➕ F7 🍴 Many 🚇 Tsim Sha Tsui ♿ Poor

TIN HAU TEMPLE

Close to the markets of Yau Ma Tei, this little temple is dedicated to Tin Hau, the goddess of seafarers. At one stage this temple looked over the har-bor. This is one of those multi-purpose temples with several other gods represented in one building.

➕ F5 ✉ Public Square Street 🕐 8am–5pm 🚇 Kowloon ♿ Poor

TSIM SHA TSUI DISTRICT

You may well be staying in this area at the southern tip of the Kowloon peninsula, as this is where many of Hong Kong's mid-range hotels are located (as well as the luxury Peninsula Hotel). There are also many shops and malls.

➕ E8 🚇 Tsim Sha Tsui 🚢 Star Ferry ♿ Good

Bustling Nathan Road

Restaurant in Tsim Sha Tsui

Symphony of Lights and a Pub Crawl

An evening stroll along the waterfront of TST followed by some of the best places to eat and drink in Kowloon. Start the walk at 8pm.

DISTANCE: 1 mile (1.5km) **ALLOW:** 45 minutes, plus drinking time

START

TSIM SHA TSUI STAR FERRY TERMINAL
⊞ E8 ⛴ Star Ferry

END

HILLWOOD ROAD
⊞ F6 Ⓜ Jordan

1 Head toward the Clock Tower (▷ 67), which is the best place to watch the Symphony of Lights (▷ 62) at 8pm. Follow the waterfront past the Hong Kong Cultural Centre (▷ 67) and the Museum of Art (▷ 55).

2 Head down the Avenue of Stars promenade (▷ 65). Take in the amazing views across the waterfront.

3 Double back toward the Space Museum (▷ 58–59) on Salisbury Road. Cross Salisbury Road via the underpass to arrive at the southern end of Nathan Road. Head north.

4 At the Chingling Mansions, turn left down Peking Road to the One Peking Road building. Head up to the top floor for a cocktail at Aqua Spirit (▷ 73).

8 The bars here have a more local feel and some strange titles.

7 Head for the district of Soho: turn right onto Observatory Road, left onto Kimberly, stay on the left onto Austin Avenue and keep an eye peeled for the stairs on the left that lead up to Hillwood Road.

6 Wander north through the park, then bear right to rejoin Nathan Road around the Kimberley Road junction. Take the next left up Knutsford Steps into Knutsford Terrace. Here you should enjoy a well-earned rest in Bahama Mama's (▷ 73) or Big Tree. This street also has a number of great restaurants that you should consider.

5 Returning down Peking Road, turn left at Hankow Road to reach Maphong Road and the southern entrance to Kowloon Park.

KOWLOON

WALK

69

Shopping

ANITA CHAN JEWELLERY

Reasonably priced and well-designed pieces, particularly interesting designs using jade and gemstones.

➕ F8 ✉ Room 1007, 10F, Harbor City, 5 Canton Road, Tsim Sha Tsui ☎ 2368 9654 🕐 Daily 9–6 🚇 Tsim Sha Tsui

BROADWAY PHOTO SUPPLY

This is the biggest branch of a Hong Kong-wide electronics and electrical chain that sells everything from washing machines to electric razors. Most major brands are available at marked down prices, which are more or less fixed, although you might get a free gift thrown in. You can get a good idea here of a sensible local price, and then move on to serious haggling in some smaller, pushier place if that's what you really want to do.

➕ E4 ✉ Ground floor & 1st floor, 731 Nathan Road, Mong Kok ☎ 2394 3827 🕐 Mon–Sat 10.30–9.30, Sun 11.30–9.30 🚇 Mong Kok

CHINESE ARTS AND CRAFTS (HK) LTD.

You can find some beautiful things here—pottery, silks, embroideries, carved gemstones, clothes, furniture, carpets, tea, jewelry, statues and novelties.

➕ E8 ✉ Star House, 3 Salisbury Road, Tsim Sha Tsui

☎ 2735 4061 🕐 Daily 10–9.30. Closed Chinese New Year 🚇 Tsim Sha Tsui

ELISSA COHEN JEWELLERY

www.elissacohen.com

This place is a bit more exciting than the standard jewelry shop chains. Lots of individually designed pieces but higher prices to match.

➕ F7 ✉ 209 Hankow Centre, 5–15 Hankow Road ☎ 2312 0811 🕐 Mon–Fri 9–5.30, Sat 9–1 🚇 Tsim Sha Tsui

FACTORY OUTLETS

The area around Granville and Kimberly roads has many factory outlets, which change names and addresses rapidly. The Hong Kong Tourist Board brochure *Factory Outlets* will have up-to-date listings.

➕ G7 ✉ Granville Road 🕐 Daily 10–9 🚇 Tsim Sha Tsui

FA YUEN STREET

Better known for its street market, this is also home

to a series of factory outlet shops. Labels are usually cut out, but you can find Marks & Spencer, Laura Ashley, Next, Saks, Victoria's Secret and many other European and US clothes at reductions of around 50 percent (or more).

➕ F4 ✉ Fa Yuen Street, Mong Kok 🕐 Daily 10–10.30 🚇 Prince Edward

FORTRESS

A major rival of Broadway, offering a similar range of cameras, sound equipment, camcorders, electronics, electronic games and so on, all at fixed prices. There are dozens of branches throughout the city, but this one is good for reconnaissance before setting off on a major haggling trip. Buy here and enjoy a hassle-free holiday, but if you like the cut and thrust of bargaining, then this should at least be your first stop.

➕ E7 ✉ Shop 333A, 333B, 335–7, 3rd floor, Ocean Centre, Harbour City, Canton Road, Tsim Sha Tsui ☎ 3101 9205 🕐 Daily 11–8.30 🚇 Tsim Sha Tsui

JUST GOLD

Popular Hong Kong chain of reasonably priced jewelry stores. Fixed prices and a bit on the kitsch side but stress-free.

➕ F7 ✉ Shop A2, 27 Nathan Road ☎ 2312 1120 🕐 Mon–Fri 11–9, Sat–Sun 10–10 🚇 Tsim Sha Tsui

CHINESE EMPORIA

Chinese emporia are perhaps the most diverse shops in the world. From markets selling knock-off goods, huge government-owned department stores selling Made-in-China basics, to private department stores stocking merchandise from around the world.

MONG KOK COMPUTER CENTRE

This small shopping block is crammed with tiny shops that spill out into the teeming corridors. The vendors are knowledgeable and catalogs of prices are on display. Hardware is mostly Asian-made: computers, monitors, printers and add-on boards. Warranties are usually only for Asia, but prices are competitive.

E4 ✉ 8–8a Nelson Street, Mong Kok 🕓 Daily 10–10 🚇 Mong Kok

OCEAN CENTRE

This and the connecting malls have branches of Carpe Diem, Francescati, Gentlemen Givenchy, Hugo, Swank Shop, as well as an excellent Marks & Spencer and local chain stores such as Giordano, G2000 and U2.

E8 ✉ Harbour City, 5 Canton Road, Tsim Sha Tsui 🕓 Daily 10–8 🚇 Tsim Sha Tsui

OPAL MINE

This is both a shop and an exhibition about opal mining and processing. Prices are low because precious stones are not taxed when imported into Hong Kong.

F7 ✉ Ground floor, Burlington House, 92 Nathan Road, Tsim Sha Tsui ☎ 2721 9933 🕓 Daily 9.30–7 🚇 Tsim Sha Tsui

RISE COMMERCIAL BUILDING

This place is filled with small boutiques carrying the handiwork of local designers, as well as affordable imports from Japan and Korea.

F7 ✉ 5–11 Granville Circuit, Tsim Sha Tsui 🕓 Various 🚇 Tsim Sha Tsui

SAM'S

www.samtailor.com

This tailor is another Hong Kong institution, numbering the Duke of Kent among its clientele.

F7 ✉ Burlington Arcade K, 92–4 Nathan Road, Tsim Sha Tsui ☎ 2367 9423 🕓 Mon–Sat 10.30–7.30, Sun 10–12 🚇 Tsim Sha Tsui

---

MADE TO MEASURE

Perhaps the most distinctive aspect of men's clothes in Hong Kong is the number and quality of tailors and the excellent prices of their products compared to almost everywhere. If you intend to have a suit made in Hong Kong, you should make finding a tailor that you like a priority, since the more time and fittings he can have the better the suit will be: a good tailor can make a suit in as little as 24 hours, but a few days will yield a better, less expensive suit. Some tailors offer a mail order service.

TSE SUI LUEN JEWELLERY (INTERNATIONAL LTD.)

There are several branches of this store around the city, selling fairly traditional designs in jewelry, watches and more. Branches in Queen's Road, Central, Causeway Bay and Nathan Road among others.

F7 ✉ Shop A&B, Ground floor, 190 Nathan Road, Tsim Sha Tsui ☎ 2926 3210 🕓 Daily 10–10.30 🚇 Tsim Sha Tsui

W. W. CHAN & SONS

Suits made by this very classy tailor have a life-span of about 20 years and will be altered free of charge during that time. Once they have taken your measurements, you can order another suit from home.

F7 ✉ A2, 2nd floor, Burlington House, 94 Nathan Road, Tsim Sha Tsui ☎ 2366 9738 🕓 Mon–Sat 9–6 🚇 Tsim Sha Tsui

YUE HWA CHINESE PRODUCTS EMPORIUM

A more basic and every-day shop than the other, more centrally located Chinese emporia. Look for inexpensive, beautiful dinner services, embroideries, pricey and inexpensive jewelry, workaday silk items and Chinese herbal medicines.

F6 ✉ 301 Nathan Road, Kowloon ☎ 3511 2222 🕓 Daily 10–10 🚇 Jordan

Entertainment and Nightlife

ALL NIGHT LONG
Newly opened live music bar in the little haven of good places to drink off Knutsford terrace.
➕ F6 ✉ 9 Knutsford Terrace ☎ 2367 9487 ⏰ Sun–Thu 4pm–5am, Fri–Sat 4pm–6am ⓂTsim Sha Tsui

AQUA SPIRIT
A quite breathtaking cocktail lounge above two of Kowloon's trendiest restaurants. The views toward Hong Kong Island are some of the best you'll see, and the music and crowd is eternally chic. An essential stop for out-of-towners.
➕ F7 ✉ 30F, 1 Peking Road, Tsim Sha Tsui, Kowloon ☎ 852 3427 2288 ⏰ Daily 5pm–2am ⓂTsim Sha Tsui

BAHAMA MAMA'S
All pub crawls on this side of the water end around here somewhere and this is as good a place as any. Nice mix of locals and gweilos. Entrance charge on club nights but worth the investment. Also the only place in Hong Kong with table football.
➕ F7 ✉ 4–5 Knutsford Terrace ☎ 2368 2121 ⏰ Mon–Thu 5pm–3am, Fri, Sat 5pm–4am, Sun 6pm–2am ⓂTsim Sha Tsui

CHILLAX BAR AND CLUB
A perennially popular spot within the increasingly established bar zone in Minden Avenue,

toward the southern end of Tsim Sha Tsui.
➕ F7 ✉ Shop G1, Ground floor, The Pinnacle, 8 Minden Avenue ☎ 2722 4338 ⏰ Mon–Thu 5pm–3am, Fri–Sat 7pm–4am, Sun 8pm–3am ⓂTsim Sha Tsui

CHUAN SPA
www.chuanspa.com
Complete with private treatment rooms and a wonderful range of luxurious products, Chuan Spa is a great place to relax. Enjoy a massage or facial in the tranquil surroundings while enjoying the serenity of the spa's waterfalls. Professional staff look after your every need.
➕ E4 ✉ Level 41, Langham Place Hotel, Mong Kok ☎ 3552 3510 ⏰ Daily 10am–11pm ⓂMong Kok

DELANEY'S
The design re-creates a Victorian Irish general store-cum-pub, and

there's live traditional music and Irish food—even Guinness. In the branch in Luard Road, there is a Sunday evening jam session.
➕ F7 ✉ Basement, Mary Building, 71 Peking Road, Tsim Sha Tsui ☎ 2301 3980 ⏰ Daily 8am–2.30am ⓂTsim Sha Tsui

HONG KONG CULTURAL CENTRE
The premier venue for orchestral music, ballet and theater. There's usually an international event of one genre or another on the schedule.
➕ E8 ✉ 10 Salisbury Road, Tsim Sha Tsui ☎ 3185 1612 ⓂTsim Sha Tsui

HONG KONG PHILHARMONIC ORCHESTRA
A large, international orchestra with regular performances, often on weekends, in the Cultural Centre (▷ 67) and City Hall. Ticket prices increase when a prestigious conductor arrives.

NED KELLY'S LAST STAND
The best place in Hong Kong for traditional and Dixieland jazz, belted out by a resident band. Expect a convivial atmosphere, pub food and no cover charge.
➕ E7 ✉ 11a Ashley Road, Tsim Sha Tsui ☎ 2376 0562 ⏰ Daily 11.30am–2am ⓂTsim Sha Tsui

Restaurants

AQUA ROMA & AQUA TOKYO ($$$)

Located on the top floor of Tsim Sha Tsui's tallest port-front tower (1 Peking Road), Aqua Roma combines Italian cuisine with panoramic views over Victoria Harbour. On the other side, Aqua Tokyo has a teppanyaki bar and booths overlooking Kowloon's gritty cityscape. The Aqua Spirit cocktail bar—the source of the Buddha Bar-style beats—is just above on the mezzanine floor.

➕ F7 ✉ 29/F, 1 Peking Road, Tsim Sha Tsui, Kowloon ☎ 3427 2288 ⏱ Mon–Sat noon–3, 6–11, Sun noon –4, 6–11

THE BOSTONIAN ($$)

Fresh fish, brought to your table for you to choose, plus imaginative preparations and bright decor suggest California—never mind the restaurant's name. If you come for the lunch buffet, plan for a light dinner.

➕ E7 ✉ Langham Hotel, 8 Peking Road, Tsim Sha Tsui ☎ 2375 1133 ⏱ Daily 12–3, 6.30–11 🚇 Tsim Sha Tsui

BULLDOG'S BAR AND GRILL ($)

Union Jacks abound in this pub and restaurant with live music nights, giant plasma screens to watch the football and a menu that includes a breakfast fry-up, fish-and-chips and more exotic dishes.

➕ G7 ✉ Shop G5, Tsim Sha Tsui Centre, 65 Mody Road ☎ 2311 6993 ⏱ Sun–Thu 11.30am–2am. Happy Hour 5–8pm 🚇 Tsim Sha Tsui

EL CID ($$)

Well-established Spanish restaurant great for a long tapas evening, but with a full Spanish menu, too. Wandering musicians serenade you as you eat. They have another restaurant in Causeway Bay.

➕ F7 ✉ Ground floor, New Knutsford House, Knutsford

DRINKS

Hotel restaurants and cafés are your best bet if you're looking for a proper English tea served with fresh milk and sugar. For decent coffee look to the European- and American-style coffee booths in glitzy shopping malls. Foreign beers and spirits are readily available—try sharp-tasting Tsingtao, Chinese beer inspired by a German recipe. If you are not used to the local beer, San Miguel, you may find it gives you a hangover. Western wine is available in most restaurants.

Terrace ☎ 2312 1898 ⏱ Mon–Sat noon–1am, Sun noon–3, 6–midnight 🚇 Tsim Sha Tsui

DAN RYAN'S CHICAGO GRILL ($$)

Traditional choices on the menu include clam chowder, potato skins, salads and baby back ribs in barbecue sauce. The burgers are universally recognized as excellent. Leave room for brownies or carrot cake. Be sure to make a reservation—this place is popular.

➕ E8 ✉ 315 Ocean Terminal, Harbour City, Tsim Sha Tsui ☎ 2735 6111 ⏱ Mon–Fri 11am–midnight, Sat–Sun 10am–midnight 🚇 Tsim Sha Tsui

DELHI CLUB MESS ($)

Plush by Chungking Mansions standards and frequented by regulars—two good reasons for a feast here.

➕ F7 ✉ Block C, Flat 3, 3rd floor, Chungking Mansions, 36–44 Nathan Road, Tsim Sha Tsui ☎ 2368 1682 ⏱ Daily 12–3.30, 6–11.30 🚇 Tsim Sha Tsui

FAT ANGELO'S ($)

For big portions, reasonable prices and home-style Italian cooking, this is the place. The lasagne easily feeds four people.

➕ F7 ✉ Shop B Basement, The Pinnacle, 8 Minden Avenue, Tsim Sha Tsui ☎ 2730 4788 ⏱ Daily noon–midnight 🚇 Tsim Sha Tsui

FELIX ($$)

You'll find excellent contemporary cuisine in this modern restaurant designed by Philippe Starck. Excellent Californian/Pan-Asian cuisine. Check out the chairs.

F8 ✉ 28th floor, Peninsula Hotel, Salisbury Road, Kowloon ☎ 2366 6251 🕔 Daily 6pm–10.30pm 🚇 Tsim Sha Tsui

FU WAH ($)

Basic decor, but very popular with the locals. No-one really speaks English, but don't worry–they do have an English menu. A wide variety of traditional Cantonese dishes and possibly the best pork and rice dishes in town. Also very good value for money so definitely worth a visit. You'll know when you're in the right street because of all the pet shops along it.

F4 ✉ 24 Victory Avenue, Kowloon ☎ 2715 6864 🕔 Daily 7am–midnight 🚇 Mong Kok KCR

GADDI'S ($$$)

One of Hong Kong's best restaurants is a place you'll remember, especially if you go at night when the chandeliers are sparkling and the band is playing. It's popular with Asian tourists for both its fine service and French food. Reservations are a must.

F8 ✉ 1st Floor, Peninsula Hotel, Salisbury Road, Tsim Sha Tsui ☎ 2366 6251 🕔 Daily 12–3, 6.30–11 🚇 Tsim Sha Tsui

GAYLORD INDIAN RESTAURANT ($)

The starters here are superb, and the breads and kebabs come fresh out of the tandoori oven. One of the best ways to try the food here is to have a lunch buffet. Cozy and pubby.

E7 ✉ 1st floor, Ashley Centre, 23–25 Ashley Road, Tsim Sha Tsui ☎ 2376 1001 🕔 Daily noon–3, 6–11 🚇 Tsim Sha Tsui

HEAVEN ON EARTH ($$)

Retro chic restaurant in Knutsford Terrace serving clever Shanghainese, Sichuan and Taiwanese cooking. Lots of spicy dishes and some excellent vegetarian options. The bar downstairs has an early-evening happy hour and both restaurant and bar are open well into the early hours.

F7 ✉ Ground floor and 1st floor, 6 Knutsford Terrace, Tsim Sha Tsui ☎ 2367 8428 🕔 Mon–Thu 4.30pm–2.30am, Fri–Sat 4.30–3.30am, Sun 4.30–1am 🚇 Tsim Sha Tsui

JIMMY'S KITCHEN ($$)

Sister restaurant to the Hong Kong Island branch, this place has been around for decades (possibly with the same furniture). Redolent of the 1920s it serves home-cooked food with a European theme, including English oysters and Russian bortsch. A Hong Kong institution.

E7 ✉ South China Building, ground floor, Kowloon Centre, 29 Ashley Road ☎ 2376 0327 🕔 Daily 11.30–2.30, 6–11 🚇 Tsim Sha Tsui

KHYBER PASS ($)

If you are keen to venture into Chungking Mansions (▷ panel), this seventh-floor mess hall is a good place to start your adventure. Seating is at long tables, prices are very low and the north Indian food is pretty standard. Clean, basic and safe.

F7 ✉ 7th floor, Block E, Chungking Mansions, Nathan Road ☎ 2721 2786 (2782 2768) 🕔 Daily noon–3.30, 6–11.30 🚇 Tsim Sha Tsui

CHUNGKING MANSIONS

To the recently arrived visitor to Hong Kong, Chungking Mansions is a scary place. The building, which houses low-cost guesthouses and eateries, heaves with people trying to sell you all manner of things, some of which you could be arrested for possessing. A few safety rules apply: Don't flash your Rolex/wallet/jewelry around. Don't hand over cash for anything unless it's in your hand.

MEZZO GRILL ($$)

American-style steaks and seafood. The restaurant specializes in char-grilled dishes. Try the sole fillets wrapped in applewood smoked bacon.

🕂 F7 ⊠ Regal Kowloon Hotel, 71 Mody Road, Tsim Sha Tsui ☎ 2313 8778 🕔 Daily 12–3, 6–11 🚇 Tsim Sha Tsui

THE MISTRAL ($$$)

Enjoy a relaxed meal away from the Tsim Sha Tsui crowds, plus excellent pasta, pizza and other Italian dishes. Rustic Mediterranean furnishings.

🕂 G7 ⊠ Basement floor 2, Grand Stanford InterContinental, 70 Mody Road, Tsim Sha Tsui ☎ 2721 5161 🕔 Daily noon–2.30, 6–10.30 🚇 Tsim Sha Tsui

NADAMAN ($$$)

The design is simple yet sophisticated, with a definite Japanese feel. There is a sushi bar available or you could reserve one of the booth tables for a more intimate meal. The extensive menu offers quality sushi, sashimi and tempura as well as other authentic Japanese cuisine. A chef's set menu is also available.

🕂 F7 ⊠ Basement floor 2, Kowloon Shangri-La, 64 Mody Road, Tsim Sha Tsui ☎ 2733 8751 🕔 Daily noon–2.30, 6–10.30 🚇 East Tsim Sha Tsui KCR, Tsim Sha Tsui MTR

SAGANO RESTAURANT ($$$)

The Japanese chefs at this restaurant in a Japanese hotel prepare distinctive kansai cuisine from around Kyoto. Don't miss the teppanyaki counter, where the chefs juggle with their cooking tools.

🕂 G7 ⊠ Hotel Nikko, 72 Mody Road, Tsim Sha Tsui ☎ 2313 4215 🕔 Daily 12–2.30, 6–10.30 🚇 Tsim Sha Tsui

SANTA LUCIA RESTAURANT AND LOUNGE ($$$)

www.hotelpanorama.com.hk Located on the 38th floor of the brand new Hotel Panorama, this excellent restaurants boasts magnificent Victoria Harbour views and a warm, intimate environment. Come for a cocktail at dusk, or enjoy the global cuisine after dark when the city sparkles. Request a window seat at all costs.

🕂 F7 ⊠ 38F, Hotel Panorama, 8A Hart Avenue, Tsim Sha Tsui ☎ 3550 026 🕔 Sun–Thu 6am–2am, Fri–Sat 6am–3am

WOODLANDS INTERNATIONAL RESTAURANT ($)

In the city's only Indian vegetarian restaurant, the decor is spare but the *dosa* (rice-flour pancakes) and *thali* (set meals) are excellent and good value. No alcohol is served here.

🕂 F7 ⊠ Upper ground floor, Wing On Plaza, 62 Mody Road, Tsim Sha Tsui ☎ 2369 3718 🕔 Daily 12–3.30, 6.30–10.30 🚇 Tsim Sha Tsui

YAN TOH HEEN ($$$)

Excellent, classy, Cantonese cuisine right on the waterfront. Gorgeous place settings in green jade. Lots of awards for its cooking and ambience. Excellent business lunch, hundreds of dim sum nibbles and 24 different types of fish on the menu.

🕂 F8 ⊠ InterContinental Hotel, 18 Salisbury Road, Tsim Sha Tsui ☎ 2721 1211 🕔 Daily noon–2.30, 6–11 🚇 Tsim Sha Tsui

---

VEGETARIAN CHOICE

Vegetarians tend to look to South Indian restaurants, which don't usually serve meat but, although meaty North Indian establishments are more common in Hong Kong, vegetarians are rarely disappointed. A couple of green vegetable dishes accompanied by *raita* (yogurt) and *naan* (puffed-up whole wheat), complemented by a lentil *dal* adds to a small feast for two.

The vast bulk of the Special Administrative Region is here in this rural hinterland north of Kowloon, studded with new towns and traditional villages, and home to some spectacular parks, walking trails, wetlands, ancient temples and museums.

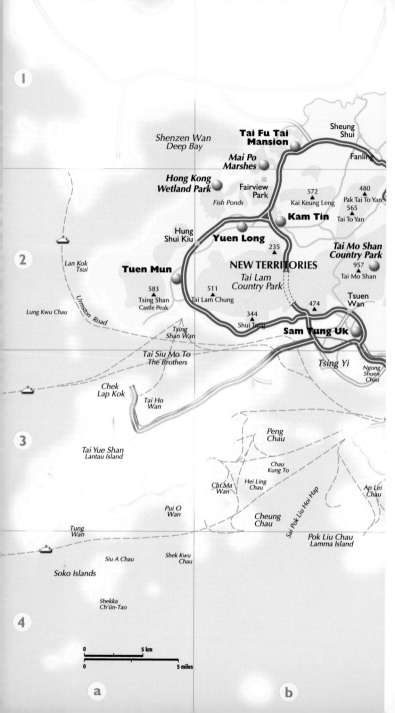

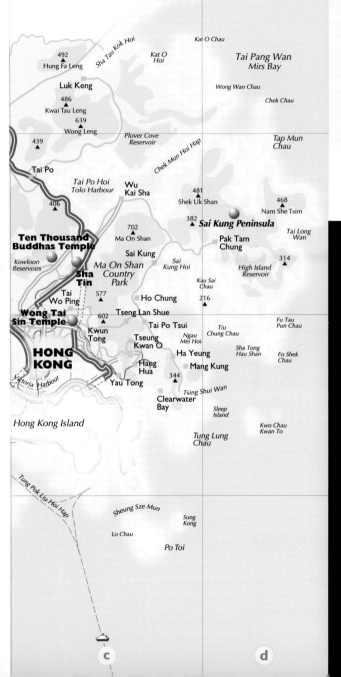

492
▲ Hung Fa Leng

Sha Tau Kok Hoi

Kat O Chau

Kat O Hoi

Tai Pang Wan
Mirs Bay

Luk Keng

Wong Wan Chau

486
▲ Kwai Tau Leng

Chek Chau

639
▲ Wong Leng

Plover Cove Reservoir

Chek Mun Hoi Hap

Tap Mun Chau

439
▲

Tai Po

Tai Po Hoi Tolo Harbour

Wu Kai Sha

481
▲ Shek Uk Shan

468
▲ Nam She Tsim

406
▲

382
▲ *Sai Kung Peninsula*

Tai Long Wan

Ten Thousand Buddhas Temple

702
▲ Ma On Shan

Pak Tam Chung

314
▲

Kowloon Reservoirs

Sha Tin

Ma On Shan Country Park

Sai Kung

Sai Kung Hoi

High Island Reservoir

Tai Wo Ping

577
▲

Kau Sai Chau

Ho Chung

216
▲

Wong Tai Sin Temple

602
▲

Tseng Lan Shue

Kwun Tong

Tai Po Tsui

Tiu Chung Chau

Fu Tau Pun Chau

HONG KONG

Tseung Kwan O

Ngau Mei Hoi

Sha Tong Hau Shan

Fo Shek Chau

Ha Yeung

Victoria Harbour

Hang Hua

Mang Kung

Yau Tong

344
▲

Tsing Shui Wan

Clearwater Bay

Sleep Island

Kwo Chau Kwan To

Hong Kong Island

Tung Lung Chau

Tung Pok Liu Hoi Hap

Sheung Sze Mun

Sung Kong

Lo Chau

Po Toi

c

d

Hong Kong Wetland Park

HIGHLIGHTS

● Pui Pui, the celebrity crocodile
● The views across the wetlands from the viewing gallery
● The wobbly mangrove boardwalk

TIPS

● The website's planner page makes your trip more productive.
● There is an indoor children's play area.

Opened to the public in May 2006, this artificial wetland area created from some disused fishing ponds now offers visitors an accessible and entertaining view of the wildlife of the Mai Po Marshes.

Wetland ecology When they undertake new developments in Hong Kong they do it on a very big scale and the Wetland Park is no exception. Lying between the Mai Po Marshes (▷ 85) and the scarily big Tin Shui Wai New Town, the wetland, all 151 acres (61ha) of it, stands as a barrier protecting the marshes from encroachment by the town and a means by which locals and visitors alike can find out about the ecology of the wetlands.

The Wetland Interactive World The visitor center isn't as boring as its title suggests. The exhibits

Tour the park on the wooden boardwalks and look out for the different kinds of plant, animal and marine life

provide information about the world's various wetlands and the impact humans have on them. The theater offers a global perspective, while the viewing gallery allows visitors to see the wetlands through telescopes and cameras located around the park.

On the boardwalks Outside, four wooden boardwalks lead visitors around the various habitats of the park: through areas planted to attract specific insects, birds, butterflies, dragonflies and mangrove dwellers, to areas for creatures that live and hunt in the streams. A floating boardwalk crosses mangroves and there are three hides where you can watch the wildlife without being seen. The reserve is home to the celebrity crocodile Pui Pui, captured in 2004 and brought here in August 2006.

THE BASICS

www.wetlandpark.com

➕ b2

✉ Wetland Park Road, Tin Shui Wai

☎ 2708 8885

🕐 Mon, Wed–Sun 10–5

🍴 Café on ground floor

🚇 KCR West route to Tin Shui Wai then light rail 705/6 Tin Shui Wai Circular to Wetland Park Station

♿ The center is accessible but boardwalks could be difficult

💲 Moderate

🏪 Shop

Ten Thousand Buddhas Temple

HIGHLIGHTS

- Thousands of small statues of Buddha
- Embalmed and gilded body of monastery's founder
- Statues of Buddha's followers
- Views over Sha Tin

TIPS

- Do not use flash photography inside the temple.
- Look out for wild macaques on the way up.

A half-hour train ride out of Hong Kong brings you to this striking temple set on a hillside overlooking the apartments, housing projects and towers of the satellite town of Sha Tin.

Bountiful Buddhas To reach the temple, take the train to Sha Tin and follow the signs. You must then climb 431 steps up the hillside. Every five steps or so is a life-size fiberglass Buddha to encourage you on your climb. Known locally as Man Fat Sze Temple, this Buddhist shrine has, since it was built between 1949 and 1957, become known as the Ten Thousand Buddhas Temple because of the matrix of small statues that decorate it. The statues, the donations of grateful worshippers over the years, are all different—some black, some covered in gold leaf—and each

There are actually many more than 10,000 Buddha statues in this temple!

Buddha strikes a different pose. There are, in fact, 13,000 or more Buddhas—but who's counting?

Panoramas and pagodas From the edge of the courtyard there are magnificent views over Sha Tin. The courtyard houses a tiered pagoda and the statues of some of Buddha's bright red followers, as well as five temples and four pavilions. Followers Manjusri and Samantabhadra occupy two of the pavilions. On the route up to the temple is another set of four temples, one containing Hong Kong's second-tallest Buddha statue, another the embalmed, gilded remains of Yuet Kai, who founded the Man Fat Sze Monastery and, despite his great age, personally carried some of the stones up to the site from the bottom of the hill. If there is a funeral taking place here, you will see paper gifts that are burned for the deceased in the afterlife.

THE BASICS

www.10kbuddhas.org (in Chinese)
➕ c2
✉ Close to Pai Tau Street, Sha Tin, New Territories
🕐 Daily 8–6. Particularly busy around Chinese New Year
🚇 Sha Tin
♿ None
💷 Free, but donations welcome

Wong Tai Sin Temple

Wong Tai Sin Temple (below left) and a streetside stand at the temple (below)

赤松黃仙祠

THE BASICS

✚ c3

✉ Wong Tai Sin Estate; follow signs from MTR station

☎ Information hotline: 2854 4333

🕐 Daily 7–5.30. Main temple is not always accessible

🚇 Wong Tai Sin

♿ Good

💰 Free, but donations welcome

HIGHLIGHTS

● Main altar including painting of Wong Tai Sin
● Garden of Nine Dragon Wall
● Fortune-telling arcade
● Clinic Block
● Stands outside selling windmills and hell money
● Chinese gardens at rear of complex
● Side altar in main temple dedicated to monkey god
● Incinerators for burning offerings

If temples were shops, then Wong Tai Sin Temple would be a supermarket. During Chinese New Year, you risk having your hair set on fire by hundreds of devotees waving joss sticks as they whirl from one deity to the next.

Wong Tai Sin This large Taoist temple, built in 1973 in Chinese style and situated among high-rise residential blocks, is dedicated to Wong Tai Sin, an ex-shepherd who was taught how to cure all ills by a passing deity. In modern-day Hong Kong, Wong Tai Sin is a very popular god, as he is in charge of the fortunes of gamblers. He can also be sought out by those who are ill or who have concerns about their health, and by people asking for help in business matters.

Symbolic interior The temple complex is vast, almost stadium-size, composed not just of the main temple, where Wong Tai Sin is represented by a painting rather than a statue, but also by turtle ponds, libraries, medicine halls and what is almost a small shopping mall of fortune-tellers. The temple is built to represent the geomantic elements of gold, wood, water, fire and earth. In the Yue Heung Shrine are fire and earth; gold is represented in the Bronze Luen Pavilion where the portrait of Wong Tai Sin is kept; and the Library Hall and water fountain represent wood and water respectively. The temple also caters to those who venerate Confucius, represented in the Confucius Hall, while Buddhists come here to worship the Buddhist goddess of mercy, Kuan Yin.

More to See

KAM TIN

The biggest of Hong Kong's clans, the Tangs, settled here hundreds of years ago, building walled villages as protection against bandits and pirates. Four hundred Tangs still inhabit the village of Kat Hing Wai.

✚ b2 ⊠ Kam Tin ⊚ Kam Sheung Road KCR ⛢ Poor

MAI PO MARSHES

On the edge of mainland China and framed by the hazy, fume-filled skyline of Shenzhen, the internationally protected Mai Po Marshes are home to thousands of rare and endangered birds—get some binoculars to view.

✚ b1 ⊠ Mai Po ☎ 2471 8272 ⊙ Daily 9–6 ⊚ Sheung Shui then a taxi 🚌 76K from Fanling KCR station ⛢ None 🕘 Moderate ❓ Reserve a visit in advance since numbers are limited. Refundable deposit required. Binoculars can be rented at the visitor center

SAI KUNG PENINSULA

This is the green lung of Hong Kong, containing the 18,772-acre (7,600ha) part of the Ma On Shan Country Park, a reservoir, the Maclehose walking trail, a marine park and the fourth highest peak in the territory. Start off at Sai Kung village, go island hopping, windsurfing or walk the trails around the park.

✚ d2 ⊙ Daily 9.30–4.30 🚌 KCR to Sha Tin then bus 299 to Sai Kung village

SAM TUNG UK

The clean, simple lines of this ancient Hakka dwelling stand out against the forest of high-rise housing blocks. Though simple farming people, the Hakka would have had far more space than their ancestors today. This translation of the village's name refers to its structure. Three connected halls form the core of village life, and the three rows of houses were supported by three central beams called *tung*. The main ancestral hall is at the front and its design is highly ornate; its original decorations have been restored to their original bright reds and greens. The other two halls, used for daily living, are more rustic. These halls now

The Sai Kung Peninsula

Women of Kam Tin in traditional Hakka dress

display farming equipment, period furniture and kitchen utensils. Outside are a fish pond, a threshing floor and the gatehouse that guarded the village.

🚹 b2 ✉ 2 Kwu Uk Lane, Tsuen Wan, New Territories ☎ 2411 2001 🕐 Mon, Wed–Sun 9–5 🚇 Tsuen Wan (exit E) 🚻 Few 🎫 Free ❓ HKTB Heritage tour, plus private tours

SHA TIN

The attractions of Sha Tin are easily visited by train from Kowloon. In addition to a huge shopping and entertainment complex, there are restaurants, temples, Hong Kong's longest and newest horse-racing track, mountain trails and a Tang walled village. Look out for the fountain opposite the station: every now and then it erupts in a special display of water and lights.

🚹 c2 🍴 Many, especially in New Town Plaza 🚇 Sha Tin KCR 🚻 Good

TAI FU TAI MANSION

Built around 1865, this traditional mansion has been fully restored; it was once home to a member of the scholar-gentry class. Ceramic figurines decorate the attractive facade, while the rooms contain plaster moldings and woodcarvings.

🚹 b1 ✉ Wing Ping, Tsuen, San Tin, Yuen Long 🕐 Daily 9–1, 2–5 🚇 Yuen Long KCR then bus 76K

TAI MO SHAN COUNTRY PARK

This country park is home to Hong Kong's highest mountain and the beautiful Ng Tung Chai waterfalls.

🚹 b2 ✉ Tsuen Wan 🍴 Take a picnic 🚇 Tsuen Wan 🎫 Free

TUEN MUN

Several interesting Buddhist and Taoist monasteries can be found in Tuen Mun, such as Castle Peak, Ching Chung Koon and Miu Fat.

🚹 a2 🚇 Tuen Mun KCR West

YUEN LONG

A one-time fishing village turned new town. Famous for the annual Tin Hau Festival and the Ping Shan hiking trail.

🚹 b2 🚇 Yeun Long KCR 🚻 Good

Red altar in the Sam Tung Uk Museum (left)

Children playng outside Tai Fu Tai Mansion (below)

To Ten Thousand Buddhas Temple

This walk from Che Kung to the Ten Thousand Buddhas Temple goes via a shopping megatropolis in Sha Tin.

DISTANCE: 2.2 miles (3.5km)   **ALLOW:** 2 hours (plus shopping time)

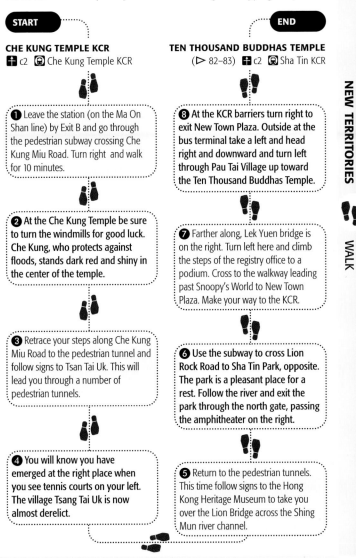

START

CHE KUNG TEMPLE KCR
✚ c2 🚇 Che Kung Temple KCR

1 Leave the station (on the Ma On Shan line) by Exit B and go through the pedestrian subway crossing Che Kung Miu Road. Turn right and walk for 10 minutes.

2 At the Che Kung Temple be sure to turn the windmills for good luck. Che Kung, who protects against floods, stands dark red and shiny in the center of the temple.

3 Retrace your steps along Che Kung Miu Road to the pedestrian tunnel and follow signs to Tsan Tai Uk. This will lead you through a number of pedestrian tunnels.

4 You will know you have emerged at the right place when you see tennis courts on your left. The village Tsang Tai Uk is now almost derelict.

END

TEN THOUSAND BUDDHAS TEMPLE
(▷ 82–83) ✚ c2 🚇 Sha Tin KCR

8 At the KCR barriers turn right to exit New Town Plaza. Outside at the bus terminal take a left and head right and downward and turn left through Pau Tai Village up toward the Ten Thousand Buddhas Temple.

7 Farther along, Lek Yuen bridge is on the right. Turn left here and climb the steps of the registry office to a podium. Cross to the walkway leading past Snoopy's World to New Town Plaza. Make your way to the KCR.

6 Use the subway to cross Lion Rock Road to Sha Tin Park, opposite. The park is a pleasant place for a rest. Follow the river and exit the park through the north gate, passing the amphitheater on the right.

5 Return to the pedestrian tunnels. This time follow signs to the Hong Kong Heritage Museum to take you over the Lion Bridge across the Shing Mun river channel.

Shopping

SHA TIN

This area out toward the racecourse is full of small electronics shops, as well as branches of the major electrical outlets. Prices are likely to be marked and fixed. You might also try the two department stores, Seiyu and Yaohan in New Town Plaza. There are lots of reasonably priced clothes shops. Don't go on Sunday or you will find yourself among what seems like the entire population of the New Territories.
➕ c2 🍴 Restaurants in New Town Plaza 🚇 Sha Tin MTR

TAI PO MARKET

This traditional market is in what was once the village of Tai Po. Stands along the main street sell everything from novelty mugs to Chinese cooking utensils and inexpensive clothes. A new air-conditioned wetmarket still sells all the strange sea creatures, fungus and herbal remedies of the old wetmarket. The two shopping malls, Uptown Plaza and Tai Po Megamall are worth a visit.
➕ c2 ✉ Tai Po 🕐 Wetmarket 6am– 9pm, malls 10am–9pm 🚇 Tai Po Market MTR

Entertainment and Nightlife

CLEARWATER BAY GOLF AND COUNTRY CLUB

A par-70, 18-hole, pro championship course. The golf course has stunning views.
➕ c3 ✉ 139 Tai Mun Road, Clearwater Bay ☎ 2719 1595 🕐 Daily 7am–9pm 🚇 Hang Hau 🏌 Green fees HK$1,800

JOCKEY CLUB KAU SAI CHAU PUBLIC GOLF COURSE

There are two 18-hole courses designed by Gary Player and a driving range at this public golf course.
➕ d2 ✉ Kau Sai Chu, Sai Kung, New Territories ☎ 2791 3388 🕐 Daily 7am–8pm 🚇 Choi Hung, then bus 92 or Green Minibus No. 1A to Sai Kung Bus Terminal. Proceed to waterfront where you board golf course's ferry for Kai Sai Cha 🏌 Green fees HK$660–HK$980

SHA TIN TOWN HALL

The large gray Town Hall at this New Territories community frequently hosts international artists, especially orchestras. To get there, exit the Sha Tin station, walk straight through the huge shopping complex and out the other side; the Town Hall is next to the library.
➕ c2 ✉ 1 Yeun Wo Road, New Town Plaza, Sha Tin ☎ 2694 2694 🕐 Daily 7am–8pm (10pm on weekends) 🚇 Sha Tin MTR

SILVERSTRAND

One of three excellent swimming beaches with changing rooms, food stalls and BBQ stations.
➕ c3 ✉ Clearwater Bay Road, Sai Kung 🚇 Choi Hung then bus 92 or taxi

Restaurants

PRICES

Prices are approximate, based on a 3-course meal for one person.

$$$	over HK$700
$$	HK$300–HK$700
$	under HK$300

ANTHONY'S CATCH ($$)

Very popular with the expatriate community, this place serves only imported seafood and stresses the freshness and source of all its seafood ingredients. Italian-style cuisine in an intimate restaurant. Live music on Thursday.

✚ c2 ✉ Ground floor lot 1826B Po Tung Road, Sai Kung ☎ 2792 8474 🕐 Mon–Sat 6pm–midnight, Sun 10.30am–4.30pm, 6pm–midnight 🚌 Choi Hung exit C2 then 1A minibus

CHUNG SHING THAI RESTAURANT ($)

Not much English is spoken in this inexpensive Thai eatery with tables outside in the street. Crowded with locals every night, the best thing to eat here is the spicy seafood.

✚ c2 ✉ 69 Tai Mei Tuk Village, Tai Po ☎ 2664 5218 🕐 9am–midnight 🚉 Tai Po KCR then bus 75K

COSMOPOLITAN CURRY HOUSE ($)

Another highly popular place in Tai Po, right beside the KCR. Loud, noisy, brash: a typical Hong Kong eatery. Food from across Asia with many inventive dishes.

✚ c2 ✉ 80 Kwong Fuk Road, Tai Po Market ☎ 2650 7056 🕐 Daily 11–11 🚉 Tai Po Market KCR

JIMMY WONG'S KITCHEN AND CAFÉ ($)

If Sha Tin New Town Plaza gets you down, wander outside to this tiny place in Pau Tai village. Surrounded by paper products shops, this air-conditioned, functional, inexpensive pan-Asian place serves home-made Japanese and Western food as well as local dishes. From Sha Tin KCR follow the signs for Ten Thousand Buddhas Temple (▷ 82–83). The café is just at the beginning of the ascent.

✚ c2 ✉ 28 Pau Tai village, Sha Tin ☎ 2601 3218 🕐 Daily 7am–10pm 🚉 Sha Tin KCR

▷ 82–83

EUROPE IN ASIA

Virtually every European cuisine is represented in Hong Kong and the food in the restaurants loses nothing from being transplanted to Asia. Local visitors like the more expensive hotel restaurants, while younger Hong Kong couples prefer the more informal European-style places.

NAM SAN GOK ($)

This Korean restaurant in New Town Plaza (▷ 89) comes well recommended by locals. Flaming traditional dishes such as Kimchee sit alongside more moderate American-influenced dishes.

✚ c2 ✉ Shop 507, Level 5, New Town Plaza Phase 1, Sha Tin ☎ 2608 2172 🕐 Mon–Fri 11.30–3.30, 5.30–11, Sat–Sun 11.30–4, 5.30–11 🚉 Sha Tin KCR

▷ 89

SAKURADA ($$)

Classy Japanese place in the Royal Park Hotel. Food is prepared by Japanese chefs and teppanyaki is a specialty.

✚ c2 ✉ 8 Pak Hok Ting Street, Sha Tin ☎ 2694 3810 🕐 Daily 11.30–3, 6–11 🚉 Sha Tin KCR

TUNG KEE SEAFOOD RESTAURANT ($–$$)

This popular Sai Kung restaurant is directly on the promenade and has plenty of outdoor tables for seaside dining on balmy evenings. It does great set meals for groups of more than two. There's a second outlet on Hoi Pong Square.

✚ c2 ✉ 96-102, Man Nin Street, Sai Kung ☎ 2792 7453 🕐 Daily 9am-11pm

Beyond Hong Kong Island itself are 260 or more outlying islands, many of them little more than uninhabited rocks, but several make for an exciting day out. One, of course, is home to the Po Lin Buddha.

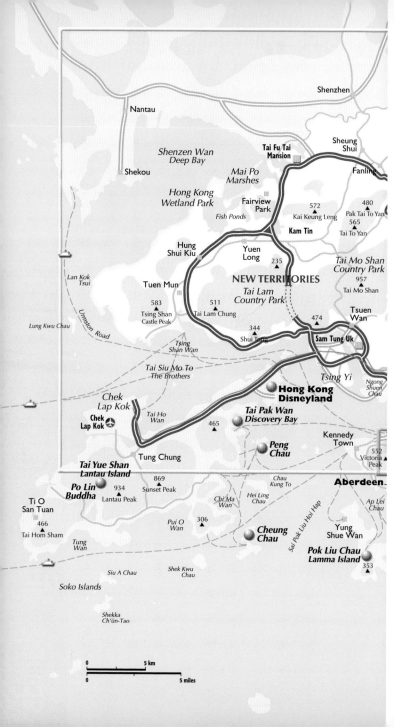

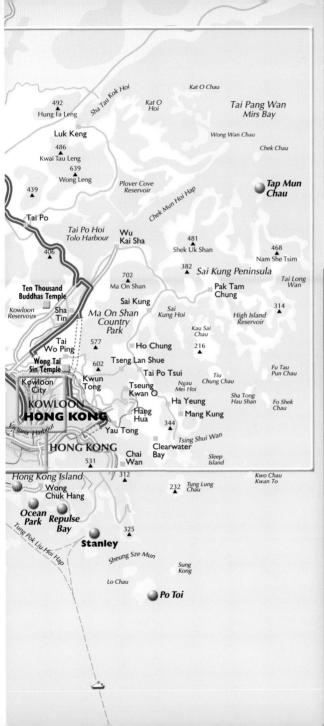

Cheung Chau Island   TOP 25

HIGHLIGHTS

- The bun festival
- Car-free walks around the island
- Sampan rides across the harbor
- Sandy beaches
- Inexpensive seafood

TIP

- The ferries from Central alternate between fast and slow—about 15 minutes difference. There is no deck access on fast ferries.

Cheung Chau has two good beaches, lots of seafood restaurants, some interesting temples, caves, windsurfing equipment and bicycles for rent, good walks, no traffic and an annual bun festival.

Ferry to Cheung Chau An air-conditioned, first-class cabin with a bar and a sunny, open-air deck make the 40-minute ferry ride past speeding catamarans, scruffy sampans, vast tankers and tiny golden islands a relaxing treat. You could spend a couple of days on this car-free island, enjoying its beaches, eating seafood and wandering the footpaths. Cheung Chau is great for scenic walks along concrete paths (watch out for the little electric vehicles that cart goods around the island). To the north, a route leads you uphill to a reservoir from where there are excellent views over the island. To

The gigantic bronze Buddha at Po Lin is a truly amazing sight

昂 NGONG
坪 PING 360

您的身心啟迪之旅由此開始
Your Journey of Enlightenment begins

restored. The monastery's real attraction is the famous Tian Tan Buddha, which was completed in 1993 on the hilltop above the monastery. To get up close, you need to climb 268 steps. At the summit, you get a splendid view of Lantau.

Footpaths and beaches Despite the new developments on the island there are still miles of quite challenging unspoiled footpaths, as well as some pretty beaches on the eastern shores, the most accessible at Mui Wo, where the ferries from Central dock. On the south coast are Pui O and Cheung Sha, both accessible from Mui Wo by bus.

Skyrail An essential part of the Lantau experience in the Ngong Ping Skyrail cable-car ride. If it's working the 3.5-mile (5.7km) ride is spectacular. Beside the upper terminus is Tang Dynasty village.

THE BASICS

✚ See map ▷ 92–93
✉ Lantau Island
🕐 Temple and museum: daily 10.30–5. Monastery: daily 9–6. Ngong Ping Skyrail Mon–Fri 10–6, Sat–Sun 10–6.30
🚇 Tung Chung and then buses heading for Po Lin or Skyrail cable-car
🚢 Ferry to Mui Wo from Outlying Ferry Pier 6 (journey time approx 45 mis)
♿ Free Skyrail moderate
❓ HKTB guided walks: Lantau Island–Tung Chung Valley

More to See

DISCOVERY BAY

A little *gweilo* enclave, "Disco" Bay, as those in the know like to call it, is a community of apartment-block dwellers, most of whom commute daily to Hong Kong Island. Enjoy car-free living and a long stretch of sandy white beaches. There are restaurants, shops and all the facilities a trendy settlement such as this requires, including the Discovery Bay Golf Club (Open by prior arrangement for non-members Monday, Wednesday and Friday), plus all the trails of Lantau to wander at will. A catamaran takes about 25 minutes from Central or buses connect with Tung Chung MTR.
✚ See map ▷ 92–93 ⛴ Air-conditioned round-the-clock ferries take 25 min from Central

LAMMA ISLAND

A short ferry ride from the city, Lamma Island is car-free and offers a relaxing day out in relatively unspoiled country-side (if you ignore the massive, ugly power station and quarrying). Most people who visit do one of the pretty, moderately simple walks and end their day with dinner in one of the island's popular seafood restaurants. Ferries arrive at the island's biggest village, Yung Shue Wan, at the north-western end of the island. There are restaurants, a bank, post office and Tin Hau temple here.

From Yung Shue Wan an hour-long, easy walk across the island brings you to Sok Kwu Wan, also accessible by ferry from Central, where the bulk of the seafood restaurants are located. Another half-hour walk from Yung Shue Wan brings you to Mo Tat Wan, a tiny village, and the nearby beaches of Shek Pai Wan and Sham Wan. From Sok Kwu Wan a path leads you to the highest point on the island, Mount Stenhouse, a stiff climb rewarded with excellent views.
✚ See map ▷ 92–93 ⛴ Outlying Islands Pier 4, Central to Yung Shue Wan: half-hourly 6.30am–12.30am. Last returning ferry at 11.30pm. From Central to Sok Kwu Wan: 7.30am–11.30pm. Last returning ferry is 10.40pm 💰 Moderate; expensive on weekends ♿ Poor

Gazing out to sea from Lamma Island

PENG CHAU

This small island to the east of Lantau is popular with day-trippers. Climb to the island's highest point, Finger Hill, at 311ft (95m), visit an 18th-century Tin Hau temple, explore the shops in the narrow lanes or sample the seafood in one of the restaurants. Five minutes from the village is Tung Wan, the island's only beach.

➕ See map ▷ 92–93 🍴 Inexpensive seafood restaurants in village ⛴ Outlying Islands Ferry Pier 6, Central: 7am–midnight. Last ferry back at 11.30pm

PO TOI ISLAND

Although close to Hong Kong Island, this tiny rocky place is one of the least accessible of the islands. Ferries run only on weekends and there is nowhere to stay on Po Toi. It is possible to visit during the week if you hire a junk. The island has a Tin Hau temple and lots of quite challenging walks. It takes about two hours to walk right round the island. Po Toi is popular with picnickers on Sunday who come for the walks and for the Bronze Age rock carving. There are a few seafood restaurants and a little beach at Tai Wan where the ferry docks. There was once a thriving village here, the only signs of which are the seafood places and some ruined houses. An excellent website www.hkoutdoors.com details a fine walk across the island.

➕ See map ▷ 92–93 ⛴ Chuen Kee Ferries operate from St. Stephen's Beach, near Stanley on Sat, Sun . Ferries also run between Aberdeen and Po Toi on Tue, Thu, Sat, Sun and public holidays

TAP MUN CHAU

A tiny island off the Sai Kung Peninsula, Tap Mun Chau has a few scattered inhabitants who make their living from fishing. There are many pleasant walks and some sandy beaches with clean water for swimming. A Tin Hau temple, some semi-wild cows and bird life make up all there is to see. On weekdays you'll have the island to yourself.

➕ See map ▷ 92–93 ⛴ 2 ferries a day (3 on Sun) from Ma Lui Shi Pier, Sha Tin. Last ferry back at 6pm (☎ 2527 2513)

A junk en route to Po Toi Island (above)

Peng Chau (right)

Lantau Island

A walk across Lantau Island from Po Lin across natural woodlands, stark hillsides and a verdant valley to the new town of Tung Chung.

DISTANCE: 4.3 miles (7km)   **ALLOW:** 3 hours

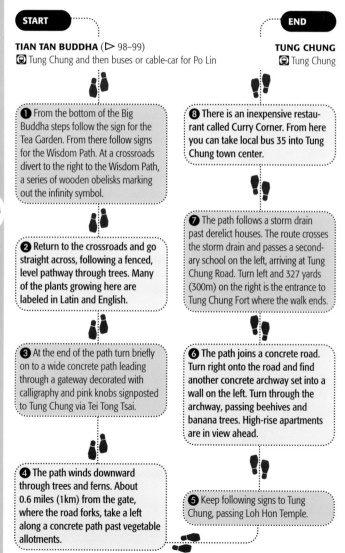

START

TIAN TAN BUDDHA (▷ 98–99)
🚇 Tung Chung and then buses or cable-car for Po Lin

END

TUNG CHUNG
🚇 Tung Chung

1 From the bottom of the Big Buddha steps follow the sign for the Tea Garden. From there follow signs for the Wisdom Path. At a crossroads divert to the right to the Wisdom Path, a series of wooden obelisks marking out the infinity symbol.

2 Return to the crossroads and go straight across, following a fenced, level pathway through trees. Many of the plants growing here are labeled in Latin and English.

3 At the end of the path turn briefly on to a wide concrete path leading through a gateway decorated with calligraphy and pink knobs signposted to Tung Chung via Tei Tong Tsai.

4 The path winds downward through trees and ferns. About 0.6 miles (1km) from the gate, where the road forks, take a left along a concrete path past vegetable allotments.

8 There is an inexpensive restaurant called Curry Corner. From here you can take local bus 35 into Tung Chung town center.

7 The path follows a storm drain past derelict houses. The route crosses the storm drain and passes a secondary school on the left, arriving at Tung Chung Road. Turn left and 327 yards (300m) on the right is the entrance to Tung Chung Fort where the walk ends.

6 The path joins a concrete road. Turn right onto the road and find another concrete archway set into a wall on the left. Turn through the archway, passing beehives and banana trees. High-rise apartments are in view ahead.

5 Keep following signs to Tung Chung, passing Loh Hon Temple.

Excursions

GUANGZHOU

The capital of Guangdong province is both the crucible of Cantonese culture and China's historic economic power-house. Concrete flyovers and tatty apartment blocks may not offer a sparkling first impression but dig a little deeper to find stunning temples, colonial relics, and China's best restaurants and markets.

THE BASICS

www.citsgd.com.cn
Distance: 75 miles (120km)
Journey Time: 2 hours (train) or 20 minutes (plane)
🚆 Express from Hung Hom
✈ From Chek Lap Kok
🛈 Yitai Square, Guangzhou

Guangzhou makes for an interesting single or two-day trip from Hong Kong. Its history can be traced back to the third century BC when the area was settled by the armies of the first Qin emperor, Qin Shi Huangdi. By the end of the first millennium AD, the city was already an international port and it became one the chief trading places as China opened up to international merchants from the 16th century.

Shamian Island is Guangzhou's most charming locale. Originally a sandbar on the Pearl River, the island was reclaimed and divided into foreign concessions after the Opium Wars of the mid-19th century. It's the only part of this ever-changing city that feels genuinely timeless.

North of Shamian is the Qingping Market. Many stalls have moved inside in beautification and hygiene campaigns. Nevertheless, the area is charming for its old-world ambience and architecture. North again is the pedestrianized shopping street of Shangxiajiu and, even farther north, is Guangzhou's most famous jade market.

West of Yuexiu Park is the Tomb of the Nanyue King, a second century BC ruler. One part of the museum re-creates the setting of the tomb though the highlight is the exhibition building.

THE BASICS

Distance: 37 miles (60km)
Journey Time: 1 hour by jetfoil

🚢 Jetfoil from the Shun Tak Centre, 200 Connaught Road 🎫 Expensive

ℹ️ Largo do Senado, Edifício Ritz No. 9, Macau
☎ (853) 315 566. In Hong Kong: Shop 336, Shun Tak Centre, 200 Connaught Road, Central ☎ 2857 2287

❓ Take your passport; no visa required for North Americans or Europeans staying 20 days or less

MACAU

Some still come to Macau for the cobbled streets, baroque architecture and traditional cuisine of Portugal's last colony (surrendered in 1999). More come to gamble in the world's new casino capital.

Macau is compact and most of the main places of interest you can take in a day. Highlights include the ruined facade of 17th-century St. Paul's Church, the Jesuit Monte Fortress and a number of old churches and temples. Hotels and good restaurants are easy to find, and prices are agreeably lower than those in Hong Kong. The things to buy here are antiques, jewelry and electrical goods. Rua de São Paulo has lots of antiques and reproduction shops, as well as stores selling Asian crafts. Largo de Senado has clothes shops where there are good bargains in woolens.

THE BASICS

www.shenzhenwindow.net
Distance: 25 miles (40km)
Journey Time: 40 min
🚆 KCR from Kowloon Tong to border at Lo Wu
❓ Single entry 5-day visas are issued at the border crossing. Visas can be obtained in advance at travel agents in Hong Kong. However, visa regulations change so please check before you finalize your travel plans.

SHENZHEN

Shenzhen is where China's capitalist experiments were first made in the 1980s. It is now China's richest metropolis. Culture is at a premium but there are also five US-style theme parks.

Here you'll find Splendid China, a theme park where the Great Wall, the Forbidden City, the terra-cotta warriors, the giant Buddha at Leshan and other monuments of Chinese art and architecture are reduced to one-fifteenth of their real size. The nearby China Folk Culture Village introduces the country's ethnic minorities.

The real draw here is the shopping—prices are significantly lower than in Hong Kong, especially for clothes, tailoring and semiprecious stones.

Shopping

LO WU COMMERCIAL CITY

Go no farther than the Chinese customs for this vast complex of shops selling, well, everything. Anything you saw and liked in Hong Kong, including last year's designer outfits at low, low prices, is probably here, all to be bargained for. Particularly good if you are considering some hand tailoring or want to buy some cloth to take back. Copies fill the shops. Take care of your personal property and bring toilet paper with you.

BARGAINING

In both Macao and Shenzhen (especially Shenzhen) some serious bargaining is in order. Visitors to Lo Wu report that shopkeepers assess your wealth before deciding at what point to make their opening bid for payment. For your own security it is important not to carry valuables in plain sight, if at all. Before you begin bargaining decide how much you want the object and how much you will pay.

➕ Map ▷ 92–93 ✉ Lo Wu 🚇 Lo Wu KCR ❓ Visas issued at border

NGONG PING VILLAGE

This village has been created as part of the Ngong Ping 360 tourism project and is designed to engender a sense of the original culture of this area. Right by the Skyrail terminal, it is an ideal spot to pick up traditional and theme souvenirs.
➕ Map ▷ 92–93
✉ Lantau Island 🚇 Tung Chung, then Skyrail

Restaurants

PRICES

Prices are approximate, based on a 3-course meal for one person.
$$$ over HK$700
$$ HK$300–HK$700
$ under HK$300

---

360 AT THE SHANGRI-LA 360 ($$$)

The cuisine and views are top-notch, to say nothing of the wine list and decor at this world-class fine-dining venue. It's just a short stroll from the Hong Kong border in Shenzhen.
➕ Map ▷ 92–93
✉ Shangri-La Hotel, 1002 Jianshe Lu, Luohu, Shenzhen ☎ 755 8396 1380 🕐 Daily 5.30–10.30

GOLDEN SIAM THAI CUISINE ($)

Just beside Tung Chung MTR en route to Ngong Ping Village and the Big Buddha at Po Lin Monastery. Surprisingly authentic food considering its touristy location.
➕ Map ▷ 92–93 ✉ Tung Chung Citygate B13 ☎ 2109 4418 🕐 11.30–5, 6–11 🚇 Tung Chung

LONG ISLAND ($$)

This place comes recommended by visitors for its lunchtime dim sum. Pleasant outdoor seating overlooking the sea. Full evening menu.
➕ Map ▷ 92–93 ✉ 52–53 Sam Hing Street, Cheung Chau ☎ 2981 1678 🕐 Daily 6am–2am 🚢 Outlying Islands Ferry Pier, Central, to Cheung Chau

TUNG YEE HEEN ($$$)

In the Mandarin Oriental in Macao. Dim sum is a specialty at lunchtime and for dinner try the spicy duck with bean-curd skin and pancakes.
➕ Off map ✉ 956–1110 Avenida da Amizade, PO Box 3016, Macau ☎ 853 8793 3821 🕐 Daily 9–2.30, 6–11

Half the fun of your stay in Hong Kong is finding and enjoying your hotel, whether it be five-star luxury or basic accommodations, where you can meet other guests and exchange travelers' tales.

Where to Stay

Introduction

Once prohibitively expensive compared to other Asian cities, Hong Kong has become quite affordable since 1997. This is partly due to the influx of Chinese tourists and the damaging effects of the various health scares in the city in the early years of the 21st century. Hong Kong hotels cater to all tastes and wallets, the seriously luxurious places being chiefly around both sides of the harbor, but sometimes also farther away from the center, while less expensive places are to be found farther north on the Kowloon peninsula.

Budget Hotels

Space is at a premium in Hong Kong so most rooms are likely to be smaller than you may be accustomed to, even if you stay in the luxury places. The really budget places are guest-houses in Tsim Sha Tsui, in some of the very old apartment blocks. Be prepared for cramped rooms, little security and few facilities, but you get to stay right at the heart of the action for very little outlay. Walk around Tsim Sha Tsui with your backpack and the guesthouses will find you.

Online Reservations

Making reservations online can save you a lot of money, with some excellent last minute deals, especially in the more expensive places. Fall (autumn) through to Chinese New Year sees reservations at their peak and this is when hotels are less likely to offer good deals. The heat of summer sees prices falling and the good deals on offer.

HOTEL TIPS

Check breakfast times before you make a reservation. Most hotels offer a bed-and-breakfast rate and the better ones could fill you up for the day. Places that offer late breakfast (say until 11am) are worth seeking out, especially if you are a night bird. If you are staying in a budget place, bring your own padlock. Some places offer lockers to store your things.

Budget Hotels

ALISAN GUEST HOUSE

http://home.hkstar.com/alisangh

These 30 rooms are on fifth floor of a block in Causeway Bay. All rooms have private showers, lavatories and air-conditioning. Friendly owners.

➕ G10 ✉ Flat A, 5th floor, Hoito Court, 275 Gloucester Road, Causeway Bay ☎ 2838 0762 🔲 Causeway Bay

BOOTH LODGE

Named after the founder of the Salvation Army (which operates the place). This hotel is well run, with clean rooms, efficient service and a small café.

➕ F5 ✉ 11 Wing Sing Lane, Yau Ma Tei ☎ 2771 9266; fax 2385 1140 🔲 Yau Ma Tei

CARITAS BIANCHI LODGE

www.caritas-chs.org.hk

Tidy, clean, well run and friendly. Laundry and restaurants are the only facilities.

➕ F5 ✉ 4 Cliff Road, Yau Ma Tei ☎ 2388 1111; fax 2770 6669 🔲 Yau Ma Tei

CARITAS LODGE (BOUNDARY STREET)

www.caritas-chs.org.hk

Basic and roomy with a coffee shop, laundry facilities and spa.

➕ G3 ✉ 134 Boundary Street, Kowloon ☎ 2339 3777; fax 2338 2864 🔲 Prince Edward, then bus 2D

GUANGZHOU GUESTHOUSE

A new and recently decorated guesthouse in the Mirador Mansion that feels slightly removed from the backpacker scrum on the floors above. It's very, very simple, and rooms are very, very small. But with air-conditioned, ensuite singles going for HK$150 it's hard to beat on price.

➕ F7 ✉ Flat B1/10F, Mirador Mansion, 54–64 Nathan Road, Tsim Sha Tsiu ☎ 2311 3085 🔲 Tsim Sha Tsui

HONG KONG HOSTEL

www.hostel.hk

The best value for budget accommodations on the island. A series of rooms

in a block of apartments, most with private bath, phone, fridge and TV. Communal kitchen.

➕ H10 ✉ Flat A2, 3rd floor, Paterson Building, 47 Paterson Street, Causeway Bay ☎ 2392 6868 🔲 Causeway Bay

NEW GARDEN HOSTEL

Mirador Mansions is fast becoming the new Chungking Mansions. Great place for meeting other backpackers and swapping stories. You have a choice of shower or bath and an open terrace. There are scores of other hostels in the same building.

➕ F7 ✉ Flat 1 E1, 13th Floor, Mirador Mansion, 58–62 Nathan Road, Tsim Sha Tsui ☎ 2311 2523; fax 2721 2085 🔲 Tsim Sha Tsui

RENT A ROOM

www.rentaroomhk.com

Businesslike place with air-conditioning, fridge, rooms with private bathrooms and some with a kitchenette. Dorm rooms and shared bathrooms make an even more economical stay. Nice area at the top of the Golden Mile.

➕ F6 ✉ 7–8 Tak Hing Street, Knight Garden Flat A, 2nd floor, Jordan ☎ 2366 3011 🔲 Jordan

Mid-Range Hotels

PRICES

Expect to pay between HK$700 and HK$2,000 per night for a mid-range hotel.

EATON

www.eaton-hotel.com
Large with a range of room rates, as well as restaurants, swimming pool, gym and a bar. Catch any bus stopping outside the door to get to Tsim Sha Tsui. Rates fall dramatically 24–48 hours before you plan to arrive.
⊞ F6 ⊠ 380 Nathan Road, Yau Ma Tei ☎ 2782 1818 ⊚ Jordan

THE EXCELSIOR

www.mandarin
oriental.com/excelsior
Pleasant and casual with nice rooms and an enormous range of facilities, right down to the two covered tennis courts on the roof. Convenient for shopping and nightlife.
⊞ G10 ⊠ 281 Gloucester Road, Causeway Bay ☎ 2894 8888 ⊚ Causeway Bay

HOTEL MIRAMAR

www.miramarhk.com
Nice location opposite Kowloon Park, all the regular room facilities—kettle, fridge, TV, etc. in large rooms for the area. This place fills up quickly so no great price reductions. Reserve in advance.
⊞ F7 ⊠ 118–130 Nathan Road, Tsim Sha Tsui ☎ 2368 1111 ⊚ Tsim Sha Tsui

HOTEL PANORAMA

www.hotelpanorama.com.hk
This brand new hotel is in a new high-rise in the thick of Tsim Sha Tsui. The design is slick and contemporary, with lots of dark woods and mirrors. There are wide harbor views, interrupted only by a couple of new tower blocks. The top floor restaurant and bar are outstanding.
⊞ F7 ⊠ 8A Hart Avenue, Tsim Sha Tsui ☎ 3550 0333 ⊚ Tsim Sha Tsui

KOWLOON HOTEL

www.harbour-plaza.com/klnh
Very modern place with many facilities but tiny rooms. Each room has its own internet connection, some have harbor views. Breakfast not included in rate.
⊞ F8 ⊠ 19–21 Nathan Road, Tsim Sha Tsui ☎ 2929 2888 ⊚ Tsim Sha Tsui

CAMPING

There are lots of places to camp in the SAR, especially in the country parks and on some of the outlying islands. The Agriculture, Fisheries and Conservation department lists 37 in the country parks, most of them very basic with toilet facilities, drains, a water supply and little more. They are mostly intended as stopping points on walks. You must bring your own equipment and in the dry season, your own water.

LAN KWAI FONG HOTEL

www.lankwaifonghotel.com.hk
Great location and excellent value at this new boutique hotel with a Chinese theme. Truly oriental decor and lots of facilities, including a gym and wireless internet. The suites are a bit more expensive but have great views over the city. The homey atmosphere here gives the place an advantage over some of the 5-star hotels.
⊞ C9 ⊠ 3 Kau U Fong, Central ☎ 2850 0899 ⊚ Central

LUK KWOK

www.lukkwokhotel.com
This is really a business-oriented hotel—no pool or views and the rooms are small—but it's good value for money and central. The rooms are all on the floors above the 19th. Two restaurants and a private cocktail bar for guests. No-smoking rooms also.
⊞ F10 ⊠ 72 Gloucester Road, Wan Chai ☎ 2866 2166 ⊚ Wan Chai

THE LUXE MANOR

www.theluxemanor.com
An eccentrically glam boutique hotel near Knutsford Terrace. There's nothing "normal" about it, from the giant wooden swing doors of the lobby, to the scarlet bins in the rooms. One for the bohemian, or fashionista.
⊞ F7 ⊠ 39 Kimberley Road,

Tsim Sha Tsui ☎ 3763 8888
🚇 Tsim Sha Tsui

MINGLE PLACE
www.mingleplace.com
This likeable new hotel makes the traditionally tiny rooms of TST seem that much bigger through a slick combination of glass, mirrors and light woods. In a quiet spott.
➕ F7 ✉ 8 Observatory Court, Tsim Sha Tsui
☎ 2377 1180

NATHAN HOTEL
www.nathanhotel.com
Big rooms in this relatively small and quiet place close to Jordan MRT. Well run, with everything you need to get by, including a babysitting service.
➕ F6 ✉ 378 Nathan Road, Tsim Sha Tsui ☎ 2388 5141
🚇 Jordan

NEWTON
www.newtonhk.com
A little way out but you get a good hotel with a Shanghainese restaurant, close to the MRT with a shuttle service to the airport, outdoor pool and internet. Small but well-appointed rooms.
➕ J9 ✉ 218 Electric Road, North Point ☎ 2807 2333
🚇 Fortress Hill

PRUDENTIAL HOTEL
www.prudentialhotel.com
A little out of the way but it has all the facilities that a 3-star hotel demands, plus a pool on the roof.
➕ F7 ✉ 222 Nathan Road, Tsim Sha Tsui ☎ 2311 8222
🚇 Jordan

ROSEDALE ON THE PARK
www.rosedale.com.hk
This is a relatively new hotel, in Causeway Bay and close to the shops. All the usual facilities in the room plus a massage service, fitness room, wireless broadband, and no-smoking rooms.
➕ H10 ✉ 8 Shelter Street, Causeway Bay ☎ 2127 8888
🚇 Causeway Bay

ROYAL PARK
www.royalpark.com.hk
Big rooms and good facilities, including a pool and a free shuttle bus into town. If you don't mind the half-hour ride into town each day, this is great value and it's close to some of the excellent walks and parks of the New Territories.
➕ Map ▷ 92–93
✉ 8 Pak Hok Ting Street, Sha Tin ☎ 2601 2111
🚇 Sha Tin KCR

CHOOSING YOUR HOTEL
Choosing a good place to stay among the hundreds of options available can be a tricky business. Websites such as **www.tripadvisor.com** have candid reviews by former guests. There can be some excellent bargains online if you are prepared to leave it to the last minute. **www.expedia.co.uk** has some good offers, while another site worth a look is **www.hongkong-hotel-guide.com**

ROYAL PLAZA
www.royalplaza.com.hk
A little way out of the center in Mong Kok this place is close to some great bargain shopping places and markets. The hotel's rather bland rooms are compensated by the lower prices that staying out of the center bring. Good Chinese restaurant and an all-day buffet in the Western restaurant. Also gym, sauna and pool with underwater music.
➕ F3 ✉ 193 Prince Edward Road West, Mong Kok
☎ 2928 8822
🚇 Mong Kok KCR

THE SALISBURY
www.ymcahk.org.hk
This 366-room YMCA is convenient for the shops and the Star Ferry. It has an inexpensive self-service restaurant and free use of a swimming pool. There are some harbor-view rooms.
➕ F8 ✉ 41 Salisbury Road, Tsim Sha Tsui ☎ 2268 7888; fax 2739 9315 🚇 Tsim Sha Tsui

STANFORD HILLVIEW
www.stanfordhillview.com
Small, quiet hotel right in the newest nightspot in town. Shuttle service to the airport train, babysitting, gym, room service, wireless broadband, bar.
➕ F7 ✉ 13–17 Observatory Road, Tsim Sha Tsui ☎ 2722 7822 🚇 Tsim Sha Tsui

Luxury Hotels

PRICES

Expect to pay more than HK$2,000 per night for a luxury hotel.

THE FOUR SEASONS

www.fourseasons.com/hongkong

This is one of Hong Kong's newest hotels. Beautifully designed with loving attention to detail, the Four Seasons offers the utmost in comfort to its guests. Restaurants, bars and a stunning rooftop swimming pool with underwater music.

⊞ C9 ✉ 8 Finance Street ☎ 3196 8888 🚇 Central

GRAND HYATT, WAN CHAI

http://hongkong.grand.hyatt.com

With amazing views over the city and large rooms the Grand Hyatt promises an enjoyable and relaxing stay. Friendly, helpful staff tend to your every need and the popular bars and restaurants may mean you never have to leave the hotel.

⊞ F10 ✉ 1 Harbour Road ☎ 2588 1234 🚇 Wan Chai

HOTEL LKF

www.hotel-lkf.com.hk

The style of this "boutique" hotel is more contemporary than its über-fashionable rivals, and rooms are unusually large for Central, starting at around 45sqm. With only 95 rooms, there's a less impersonal feel than at the larger five-stars in the area and there are great views from upper floors. The wining and dining on the 29th and 30th floors is spectacular.

⊞ E9 ✉ 33 Wyndham Street, Central ☎ 3518 9688 🚇 Central

INTERCONTINENTAL HONG KONG

www.hongkong-ic.intercontinental.com

Simple, elegant place, with good *feng shui*. Some of the best views across the harbor to the island. Amazing swimming pool. Award-winning Cantonese restaurant.

⊞ F8 ✉ 18 Salisbury Road, Tsim Sha Tsui ☎ 2721 1211 🚇 Tsim Sha Tsui

ISLAND SHANGRI-LA

www.shangri-la.com

Towering above Central with amazing views over the city this luxurious hotel has spacious, well-designed rooms, some great places to eat and drink, and the world's longest Chinese painting. Good fitness suite and pool. Library for guests.

⊞ E11 ✉ Pacific Place, Supreme Court Road, Central ☎ 2877 3838 🚇 Central

LANGHAM PLACE HOTEL

http://hongkong.langham-placehotels.com

The only 5-star hotel in Mong Kok, Langham Place has a very impressive line-up of guest facilities with flat-screen TVs, huge rooms with enormous marble tile bathrooms, great service from a dedicated staff and best of all, a really good spa complete with private treatment rooms and all kinds of health and beauty treatments.

⊞ E4 ✉ 250–555 Shanghai Street, Mong Kok ☎ 3552 3388 🚇 Mong Kok

MANDARIN ORIENTAL

www.mandarinoriental.com/hongkong

The very central Mandarin Oriental has a long tradition of impeccable service. Well-appointed rooms, with superb attention to detail. Helpful staff, classy shops, great pool, excellent restaurants. It has reopened after a huge refit and is looking better than ever.

⊞ D10 ✉ 5 Connaught Road, Central ☎ 2522 0111 🚇 Central

ISLAND OR KOWLOON?

For top-notch hotels in Hong Kong you should decide whether you want to stay on the island or in TST. Some of the hotel chains, such as Shangri-La, have hotels in both areas and most of them have amazing views across the harbor. If you love to stay in your room, then TST is the best for its better views of the nightly Symphony of Lights but if you're a nightlife lover then the island is the place for you.

This section offers all you need to know about Hong Kong, from how to pay your tram fare to where to go to send an e-mail, to opening hours and health precautions—all the ins and outs of a visit.

Need to Know

Planning Ahead

When to Go

The ideal time to visit is between October and mid-December, when the days are warm and fresh and the nights are cool. Try to avoid June through September, when the weather is extremely hot and humid. The hotels are at their most expensive from late fall to early February.

NEED TO KNOW   PLANNING AHEAD

AVERAGE DAILY MAXIMUM TEMPERATURES

JAN	FEB	MAR	APR	MAY	JUN	JUL	AUG	SEP	OCT	NOV	DEC
64°F	63°F	66°F	75°F	82°F	84°F	88°F	88°F	84°F	81°F	73°F	68°F
18°C	17°C	19°C	24°C	28°C	29°C	31°C	31°C	29°C	27°C	23°C	20°C

Spring (March through May) is usually warm, although rain is common.
Summer (June through September) is very hot and humid, with nearly 16in (400mm) of rain on average each month. The clammy heat sometimes gives way to violent typhoons.
Fall (October through to mid-December) is usually warm.
Winter (mid-December through February) is comfortable, with occasional cold spells.
Typhoons hit between July and September. Hotels post the appropriate storm signal: Storm Signal 1=Typhoon within 500 miles (800km) of Hong Kong; Storm Signal 3=Typhoon on its way, be prepared; Storm Signal 8=Stay in your hotel, dangerous winds with gusts.

WHAT'S ON

January/February *Chinese (Lunar) New Year*: This family event looms large in Hong Kong life. The week before the New Year is busy; the harbor fireworks display is magnificent, but the crowds are enormous.
Mid-February/mid-March *Arts Festival*: International orchestral, dance and theater events over four weeks.
March *Hong Kong Sevens*: This rugby tournament is a wild three-day-long expat party.
Late March/April *International Film Festival*:

For two weeks; various venues.
April *Ching Ming*: Tomb-sweeping day.
Tin Hau Festival: Tin Hau temples remember a 12th-century legend about a girl who saves her brother from drowning. Fishing junks and temples are decorated and Chinese street operas held near the temples.
Birthday of Lord Buddha (late April): At temples Buddha's statue is ceremonially bathed and scented symbolically washing away sins and material encumbrances.

May/June *Dragon Boat Festival*: Noisy, colorful dragon-boat races are enthusiastically held to commemorate the political protests of a 4th-century poet and patriot, Chu Yuan.
August/September *Hungry Ghosts Festival*: Offerings of food are set out to placate roaming spirits.
September/October *Mid-Autumn Festival*: Families head out with lanterns and eat mooncakes to commemorate the fullest moon of the year.

Hong Kong Online

www.discoverhongkong.com
The official website of the Hong Kong Tourist Board. General information about Hong Kong, suggestions for day trips, family days out, history, information on transport, etc.

www.bcmagazine.net
The website of the free magazine of the same name. Lots of information on what's on, restaurant reviews, shopping tips, all aimed at a young audience.

www.gayhk.com
Information about Hong Kong's gay scene, attitudes in the territory, good places to visit, reviews of clubs, bars and more.

www.scmp.com.
This is the site of the *South China Morning Post*, the territory's independent newspaper. News items, cultural information, current affairs. Gives an insight into what concerns Hong Kongers.

www.thestandard.com.hk
Breaking news from Hong Kong's second English-language newspaper. Unlike rival SCMP (above), all content can be accessed for free.

www.skybird.com.hk
Information and prices for tours of this accredited travel agency in the city.

www.grayline.com.hk
A well-established tour company gives details of tours of the island and trips into China.

www.hongkongairport.com
The site of Hong Kong International Airport with useful information before you actually arrive.

www.hkclubbing.com
This site keeps track of the new and not so new clubs in the city.

NEED TO KNOW PLANNING AHEAD

USEFUL WEBSITES

www.fodors.com
A complete travel-planning site. You can research prices and weather; reserve air tickets, cars and rooms; ask questions (and get answers) from fellow visitors; and find links to other sites.

www.mtr.com.hk
Information on the metro system in Hong Kong. Details of Octopus cards, airport express, tourist passes, many other useful details.

www.tripadvisor.com
Website selling hotel deals, which has reviews by visitors, many of them very candid.

INTERNET CAFÉS

Hong Kong Central Library
🔒 H9 ✉ 66 Causeway Road, Causeway Bay
☎ 3150 1234 🕐 Tue–Thu 10–9, Wed 1pm–9pm
👆 Free

Pacific Coffee Company
This mega-chain has outlets across the SAR.
🔒 F7 ✉ Miramar Shopping Centre G31–32A, 132 Nathan Road, Tsim Sha Tsui ☎ 2735 0112
🕐 Mon–Thu 7am–midnight, Fri, Sat 7am–1am, Sun 8am–midnight 👆 Free with purchase of coffee

Getting There

ENTRY REQUIREMENTS

All visitors must hold a valid passport. For the latest passport and visa information, look up the website www.immd.gov.hk

VISITORS WITH DISABILITIES

Generally speaking wheelchair users will find that the newer buildings have good access while older buildings and most streets, MTR stations, footbridges, of which there are hundreds, and shopping centers are difficult to negotiate. Taxis, ferries and some buses are wheelchair friendly.

Joint Council for the Physically and Mentally Disabled

✚ Room 1204, 31 Hennessy Road, Wan Chai, ☎ 2864 2931, www.hkcss.org.hk

AIRPORTS

All flights land at Hong Kong International Airport at Chek Lap Kok 15 miles (24km) west of Hong Kong city. The eight floors of the airport include three banks, a moneychanger, several ATMs, a tourist information office and acres of restaurants and bars.

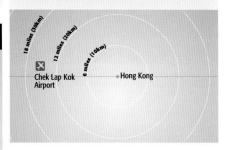

Chek Lap Kok Airport   • Hong Kong

ARRIVING AT CHEK LAP KOK AIRPORT

For airport information ☎ 2181 0000; www.hkairport.com.

The Airport Express (☎ 2881 8888; www.mtr.com.hk) is the most efficient and pleasant way of getting to town from the airport. Trains depart for the city at 12-minute intervals from 5.50am to 12.48am; journey time to Central is 24 minutes, to Kowloon 18 minutes; cost HK$100 one way to/from Central, HK$90 to/from Kowloon. A same-day return is the same as a single fare.

There are also bus services into Hong Kong Island, Kowloon, the New Territories and Lantau Island, which are less expensive. Information on times and prices can be obtained from the tourist office in the airport or www.citybus. com.hk. The Citybus A11 travels into Hong Kong Island for HK$40, while the A21 serves Kowloon for HK$33.

A taxi to Hong Kong Island is the expensive option and will cost around HK$340. This includes the toll fare for the Lantau Link, the bridge that joins Lantau Island to Hong Kong Island. The journey to Kowloon costs around HK$270.

ARRIVING BY BUS

Bus services from Shenzhen and a host of Pearl River Delta (Guangdong) cities are provided by CTS Express coaches. There are buses to downtown stops and direct buses to the airport.
✉ Room 209 KCRC Hung Hom Building, 8 Cheong Wan Road, Hung Hom ☎ 2764 9803. To travel into China you must get a visa in advance of your journey.

ARRIVING BY TRAIN

High-speed trains travel from Guangzhou East railway station to Hung Hom 12 times a day 8.35am–9.23pm. There are also rail links with Shanghai and Beijing.

EMBASSIES AND CONSULATES

● **Australia** ✉ 23rd and 24th Floors, Harbour Centre, 25 Harbour Road, Wan Chai ☎ 2827 8881
● **Canada** ✉ 11th–14th floors, Tower One, Exchange Square, 8 Connaught Place, Central ☎ 2810 4321
● **Germany** ✉ 21st floor, United Centre, 95 Queensway, Central ☎ 2105 8788
● **UK** ✉ 1 Supreme Court Road, Admiralty ☎ 2901 3000
● **US** ✉ 26 Garden Road, Central ☎ 2523 9011

Getting Around

SENSIBLE PRECAUTIONS

● Hong Kong is very crowded, night and day, and professional thieves capitalize on this.
● Keep wallets and purses secure.
● Keep traveler's checks separate from the invoice that lists their numbers.
● Don't leave valuables where you can't see them at all times.
● Keep travel documents and money in a hotel safe.

Lost Property
✉ Admiralty MTR station
🕐 Mon–Sat 8–7
☎ 2861 0020

TOURIST INFORMATION

● The Hong Kong Tourist Board (HKTB) has three downtown offices:
✉ Star Ferry Concourse, Tsim Sha Tsui 🕐 Daily 8–8
✉ Causeway Bay MTR
🕐 Daily 8–8
✉ Peak Piazza 🕐 Daily 9–9
● Visitor Hotline:
☎ 2508 1234, daily 8–6
● The tourist board has developed the Quality Tourism Services scheme Look for the QTS logo.

SKYRAIL

● Skyrail is an aerial cable-car linking Tung Chung with Ngong Ping on Lantau Island.

TRAINS

● The MTR (Mass Transit Railway) is the quickest way to hop between shopping areas, between Hong Kong Island and TST; for access to the New Territories use the interchange station at Tsim Sha Tsui or Kowloon Tong and change to the KCR (Kowloon Canton Railway), which travels north to the border at Lo Wu.
● Stations have clear instructions in both English and Chinese for operating ticket machines. Machines issue thin plastic cards that are also available from information/ticket counters. Fares are between HK$3 and HK$36.5. Tickets have a magnetic strip and the fare is deducted automatically as you pass through the ticket barrier ☎ 2881 8888.
● MTR maps are available at the airport and most hotel lobbies. MTR stations dispense a free guide to the system in English and Chinese.

BUSES

● Traveling on buses is not really recommended (except for trips to the south side of Hong Kong Island), but in the event of using one, note the fixed fare is marked on the bus as you enter and pay; no change is given. The MTR train network is faster and easier to use. Tourist Board offices have a free map showing bus fares and routes.

TAXIS

Taxis are good value and can be picked up at ranks, although many drivers do not speak English. Once inside you must use the seat belt.
● The flagfare is HK$16 and after a 1.5-mile (2km) the fare increases by HK$1.40 for every 210 yards (200m). There is a HK$5 additional charge if a taxi is reserved by phone and comes to your pick-up point. An additional charge of HK$5 may be made for each large piece of baggage. Fares might be slightly different in the New Territories and Lantau.
● A "For Hire" sign is displayed in the windscreen; at night a "Taxi" sign is lit up on the roof.

● Taxis are not supposed to stop at bus stops or on a yellow line.

TRAMS
● Trams run only on Hong Kong Island's north side—the route between Kennedy Town in the west and Causeway Bay in the east is useful.
● Destinations are marked on the front in English.
● The fixed fare of HK$2 is dropped in the pay-box when leaving the tram.

THE OCTOPUS CARD
If your stay in Hong Kong is an extended one you might want to consider buying an Octopus Card (HK$150). This is a prepaid card that can be used on most of the city's transport systems, but is also coming into use in shops and other businesses to replace cash. The card is not per-sonalized and the HK$100 deposit is refund-able. The drawback to the card of course is that it operates in the same way as cash and can be stolen as easily. The balance of cash on the ticket can be checked each time you use it.

ORGANIZED SIGHTSEEING
● The **Hong Kong Tourist Board** (▷ 118) conducts tours to a number of destinations, as well as lots of theme tours.
● **Splendid** organizes personalized tours of Hong Kong and South China, including an Aberdeen or harbor night cruise, horse racing (June–September), Lantau Island and a Splendid Night of delight. They also do tours into China (☎ 2316 2151; www.splendidtours.com ▮ HK$280).
● **Water Tours Ltd**. conducts nearly 20 different harbor cruises, including a Sampan ride around Aberdeen (☎ 2926 3868; www.watertours.com.hk).
● **Star Ferry** runs six to eight harbor tours a day (☎ 2366 7024; www.starferry.com.hk).
● **Grayline Tours** offers city tours, dinner cruises and day trips to China (☎ 2368 7111; www.grayline.com.hk).

LONE TRAVELERS
● Hong Kong is similar to, and often safer than, European or North American cities; take commonsense precautions.
● Public transportation at night is as safe as during the day.

STUDENT TRAVELERS
● There are few discounts for ISIC (International Student Identity Card) holders.
● The Student Travel Bureau ✉ Room 1021, 10/F, Star House, Tsim Sha Tsui ☎ 2730 3269 🕐 9.30–6 dispenses a free booklet detailing retail outlets with student discounts.
● Some places of interest have a reduced student admission.

EMERGENCY NUMBERS
● Police/Fire/Ambulance ☎ 999

THE MID LEVELS
● Special to Hong Kong is the 15-minute trip up to the Mid Levels on escalators. The series of escalators begins in Central, on Des Voeux Road, and extends up through the residential tiers in hilly Central.

Essential Facts

OPENING HOURS

- Offices: Mon–Fri 9–5, Sat 9–1
- Banks: Mon–Fri 9–4.30, Sat 9–12.30
- Post offices: Mon–Fri 9.30–5, Sat 9.30–1
- Shops: Daily 10–6, often 10–9/11–10 in tourist areas.

MONEY

The unit of currency is the Hong Kong dollar (= 100 cents). Notes comes in denominations of 10, 20, 50, 100, 500 and 1,000; coins are 10, 20 and 50 cents.

50 dollars

100 dollars

500 dollars

1000 dollars

ETIQUETTE

- Hong Kong is a fast city so don't be surprised when people push, shove and jump the line or fail to line up at all.
- Shaking hands is common practice, as is the exchanging of business cards, presented with both hands.
- A service charge is usually added to restaurant bills, but the staff do not get this money as tips so an extra 10 percent is expected. Round up taxi fares to the next dollar or two.

MEDICAL TREATMENT

- Outpatient departments of public or private hospitals provide emergency treatment.
- Private doctors (see Yellow Pages) charge HK$150 per visit on average. This usually includes three days' medication.
- **Public hospitals:**

Queen Mary Hospital ✉ Pok Fu Lam Road, Hong Kong Island ☎ 2855 3838

Queen Elizabeth Hospital ✉ Wylie Road, Yau Ma Tei, Kowloon ☎ 2958 8888

Kwong Wah Hospital ✉ 25 Waterloo Road, Yau Ma Tei, Kowloon ☎ 2332 2311

- **Private hospitals:**

Hong Kong Central ✉ 1 Lower Albert Road, Central, Hong Kong Island ☎ 2522 3141

Adventist ✉ 40 Stubbs Road, Wan Chai, Hong Kong Island ☎ 2574 6211

Baptist ✉ 222 Waterloo Road, Kowloon Tong ☎ 2339 8888

MONEY MATTERS

- Traveler's checks can often be used as payment or cashed at banks or moneychangers. Always check the exchange rate before making any transaction; banks offer the best rates. There are scores of small streetside moneychangers (particularly in Tsim Sha Tsui and Causeway Bay). It's safe to change cash here, though shop around for the best deal as rates vary.
- Credit cards—Visa, Access (MasterCard), American Express and Diners Club—are widely

accepted for purchases in shops and restaurants. In small shops check commission is not added—this is illegal.

● Credit cards can be used to obtain cash from banks and ATM machines. Some Hong Kong Bank teller machines provide 24-hour HK$ withdrawal facilities for Visa and MasterCard holders. Amex holders have the same facility at some Jetco ATMs, as well as the Express ATMs.

NATIONAL HOLIDAYS

Dates of the Chinese lunar festivals vary from year to year.
● 1 January: New Year's Day.
● Late January or early February: Chinese New Year (three days).
● Good Friday and Easter Monday.
● Early April: Ching Ming Festival.
● 4 April/early May: Buddha's birthday.
● 1 May: Labor Day.
● Mid- to late-June: Dragon Boat Festival.
● 1 July: Hong Kong SAR Establishment Day.
● Late September or early October: Mid-Autumn Festival.
● 1 October: China National Day.
● Mid- to late October: Cheung Yeung Festival.
● 25 and 26 December: Christmas Day and Boxing Day.

NEWSPAPERS AND MAGAZINES

● International newspapers and magazines are available in bookstores, hotel kiosks and newsagents on street corners. The newsagent outside the Star Ferry terminal in Tsim Sha Tsui and the bookstore next to the ferry terminal in Central have a good selection.
● There are two English-language daily newspapers: the broadsheet *South China Morning Post* and the tabloid *Hong Kong Standard.*
● For entertainment listings look for the free, bi-weekly *HK Magazine* or *BC Magazine.*

TOILETS

● Most are Western style.
● Hotels are the best places to find clean toilets.
● In older places, on public transportation, toilets are often the squat type.
● Public toilets are free.
● Always carry a packet of tissues.

ELECTRICITY

● The current is 200/220 volts, 50 cycles alternating current (AC).

● Most wall outlets take three square prongs; some older ones take three large round prongs.

● US appliances require a converter and a plug adaptor.

PLACES OF WORSHIP

● **Protestant Evangelical Community Church** ✉ 4th floor YMCA, Salisbury Road, Tsim Sha Tsui ☎ 2369 2211

● **The Roman Catholic Cathedral** ✉ 16 Cairn Road, Mid Levels, Hong Kong Island ☎ 2810 4066

● **Jewish Ohel Leah Synagogue** ✉ 70 Robinson Road, Central ☎ 2857 6095

● **Kowloon Mosque** ✉ Kowloon Park ☎ 2724 0095

POST OFFICES

The General Post Office on Hong Kong Island is at 2 Connaught Place, Central.

● In Kowloon, the main post office is at the ground floor of the Kowloon Government Offices, 405 Nathan Road, Yau Ma Tei. There is also the International Mail Centre Post Office at 80 Salisbury Road.

● Letters and postcards to destinations outside Southeast Asia cost HK$5.30 for up to 30g, plus HK$1.30 for each additional 10g.

● The Speedpost service (☎ 2921 2277) cuts the usual five-day service to Europe or North America by about half.

TELEPHONES

● Local calls are free from private homes. Public phones charge HK$1 per call and sometimes only take HK$2 coins without giving change. Pressing the "FC" (follow-on call) button before hanging up allows a second call.

● Phonecards, available in denominations of HK$50 and HK$100 at 7–Eleven stores and other shops, are easier to use, especially for International Direct Dialling calls.

● Some telephone boxes accept only phonecards or only coins.

● For IDD calls, dial 001, followed by the country code and then the area code (minus any initial 0) and number. Dial 013 for information about international calls.

● To call Hong Kong from abroad dial 00 852, then the 8-digit number.

Language

Hong Kong has two official languages: Cantonese and English. While English is spoken widely in business circles and tourist areas, it is not always understood elsewhere. It's best to get the hotel receptionist to write down your destination in Chinese. A few words of Cantonese go a long way in establishing rapport—and off the beaten track they may prove useful.

BASICS	
neih wuih mwuih gong ying mahn?	Can you speak English?
jóu sahn	good morning
néih hou ma?	how are you?
wai! (pronounced 'why')	hello (only on the phone)
mgòi	thank you (for a favor)
dò jeh	thank you (for a gift)
mgòi	please
mgòi	excuse me
deui mjyuh	I'm sorry
haih or hou	yes
mhaih or mhou	no
bin douh?	where?
fèi gèi chèung	airport
bā si	bus
dihn chè	tram
géi dō?	how many/how much?
géi dō chin?	how much is it?
géi dim jung?	what time is it?

NUMBERS	
leng	0
yāt	1
yih	2
sàam	3
sei	4
ngh	5
luhk	6
chát	7
baat	8
gáu	9
sahp	10
sahp yāt	11
yih sahp	20
yih sahp yāt	21
saam sahp	30
sei sahp	40
ngh sahp	50
luhk sahp	60
chát sahp	70
baat sahp	80
gáu sahp	90
gáu sahp gáu	99
yāt baak	100
yāt chihn	1000

Timeline

4000BC Early settlement left some pottery, stone tools and iron implements—then for many centuries the islands had more pirates than farmers.

c200BC The Chinese Empire is unified and for the next millennium-and-a-half Hong Kong Island is ruled by a governor based in Canton.

1685 British and French merchants begin to deal in tea and silk. The British later start to import opium as a way of extending their power and profits.

1839–42 Chinese attempts to block the import of opium end in defeat; the treaty concluding the first Opium War cedes Hong Kong Island to the British "in perpetuity." Within two decades, another treaty concedes the Kowloon Peninsula. In 1889 a further treaty leases substantial land north of Kowloon—the New Territories—to Britain for 99 years.

1941–45 Japanese occupation (▷ panel this page).

1949 The Communist victory in China leads to refugee influxes.

1950–53 When the US imposes sanctions against China during the Korean War the colony develops a manufacturing base of its own.

Former government building Murray House; an old post box; Lei Cheng Uk Museum; a flag-raising ceremony; Golden Bauhinia next to Hong Kong Convention Centre (left to right)

1967 The political passions rocking China spill over into Hong Kong, with riots and strikes. The colony seems on the brink of a premature closure of its lease, but normality soon returns.

1975 100,000 Vietnamese refugees arrive.

1982 British Prime Minister Margaret Thatcher goes to Beijing to discuss the colony's future.

1984 The Sino-British Joint Declaration confirms the return of the colony to China. In 1988 Beijing publishes its Basic Law for Hong Kong citizens, guaranteeing their rights.

1989 The Tiananmen Square massacre confirms Hong Kong's worst fears about the future under China's sovereignty. More than one million people protest on the streets of Hong Kong.

1997 Hong Kong becomes a Special Administrative Region of China. English remains an official language. People from other parts of China require special approval for entry.

1998 Turmoil in Asian stock markets delivers a blow to Hong Kong.

2003 SARS epidemic disrupts life on the island.

2007 Tenth anniversary of the Handover.

THE HANDOVER

At midnight on 30 June 1997, Britain's last vestige of empire was handed back to the Chinese. Trepidation surrounded the occasion, but in the event it was a muted affair in one of the worst rainstorms in memory. Few people were on the streets. Chris Patten, Hong Kong's last governor, and Prince Charles quietly and tearfully slipped away on the royal yacht Britannia and the Red Army silently drove across the border. The expatriate workers who had not chosen to leave marked the occasion in Lan Kwai Fong bars, and everyone woke up the next day a little nervously, wondering how their lives would be changed, and a little shocked that nothing seemed different.

NEED TO KNOW TIMELINE

Index

Hong Kong's
25 Best

WRITTEN BY Joseph Levy Sheehan
UPDATED BY Graham Bond
DESIGN WORK Jacqueline Bailey
COVER DESIGN Tigist Getachew
INDEXER Marie Lorimer
IMAGE RETOUCHING AND REPRO Michael Moody and Sarah Montgomery
EDITOR Bookwork Creative Associates
REVIEWING EDITOR Linda Cabasin
SERIES EDITOR Marie-Claire Jefferies

ISBN 978-1-4000-0378-5

SIXTH EDITION

IMPORTANT TIP
Time inevitably brings changes, so always confirm prices, travel facts, and other perishable information when it matters. Although Fodor's cannot accept responsibility for errors, you can use this guide in the confidence that we have taken every care to ensure its accuracy.

SPECIAL SALES
This book is available for special discounts for bulk purchases for sales promotions or premiums. Special editions, including personalized covers, excerpts of existing books, and corporate imprints, can be created in large quantities for special needs. For more information, write to Special Markets/Premium Sales, 1745 Broadway, MD 6–2, New York, NY 10019 or email specialmarkets@randomhouse.com.

Color separation by Keenes, Andover, UK
Printed and bound by Leo Paper Products, China
10 9 8 7 6 5 4 3 2 1

A03803
Maps in this title produced from mapping © MAIRDUMONT / Falk Verlag 2009 and map data supplied by Global Mapping, Brackley, UK. © Global Mapping Transport map © Communicarta Ltd, UK

The Automobile Association would like to thank the following photographers, companies and picture libraries for their assistance in the preparation of this book.

Abbreviations for the picture credits are as follows: (t) top; (b) bottom; (l) left; (r) right; (AA) AA World Travel Library.

1 Hong Kong Tourism Board; 2-18 AA/B Bachman; 4tl AA/B Bachman; 5 AA/B Bachman; 6cl AA/B Bachman; 6c AA/N Hicks; 6cr AA/B Bachman; 6br Photodisc; 7tl AA/B Bachman; 7tcl AA/B Bachman; 7tcr Hong Kong Tourism Board; 7tc Hong Kong Tourism Board; 7cl Hong Kong Tourism Board; 7c AA/B Bachman; 7cr AA/B Bachman; 10tr AA/B Bachman; 10tcr AA/B Bachman; 10/11c AA/B Bachman; 10/11b AA/B Bachman; 11tl AA/B Bachman; 11tcl AA/N Hicks; 12b AA/B Bachman; 13 (i) AA/B Bachman; 13 (ii) AA/B Bachman; 13 (iii) AA/B Bachman; 13 (iv) AA/B Bachman; 13(v) AA/B Bachman; 14tr AA/B Bachman; 14tcr AA/B Bachman; 14cr AA/B Bachman; 14br AA/B Bachman; 16tr A Mockford & N Bonetti; 16cr AA/B Bachman; 16br Hong Kong Tourism Board; 17tl Hong Kong Tourism Board; 17tcl AA/D Henley; 17cl Hong Kong Tourism Board; 17bl Hong Kong Tourism Board; 18tr Leisure and Cultural Services Department of Hong Kong Special Administrative Region Government; 18tcr Stockbyte Royalty Free; 18cr Ocean Park Hong Kong; 18br AA/B Bachman; 19 (i) AA/B Bachman; 19 (ii) Hong Kong Tourism Board; 19 (iii) AA/B Bachman; 19 (iv) AA/B Bachman; 20 Hong Kong Tourism Board; 24l AA/B Bachman; 24/25t AA/B Bachman; 24/25c AA/B Bachman; 25t AA/B Bachman; 25cl AA/B Bachman; 25cr AA/B Bachman; 26l Leisure and Cultural Services Department of Hong Kong Special Administrative Region Government; 26/27t Leisure and Cultural Services Department of Hong Kong Special Administrative Region Government; 26/27c Leisure and Cultural Services Department of Hong Kong Special Administrative Region Government; 27t Leisure and Cultural Services Department of Hong Kong Special Administrative Region Government; 27c Leisure and Cultural Services Department of Hong Kong Special Administrative Region Government; 28tl AA/D Henley; 28tc AA/N Hicks; 28tr AA/N Hicks; 29tl AA/A Kouprianoff; 29tr AA/A Kouprianoff; 30tl AA/A Kouprianoff; 30tr AA/N Hicks; 31tl AA/A Kouprianoff; 31tr AA/Nicks; 32tl Ocean Park Hong Kong; 32tr Ocean Park Hong Kong; 32cl Ocean Park Hong Kong; 32cr Ocean Park Hong Kong; 33t Ocean Park Hong Kong; 33cl Ocean Park Hong Kong; 33cr Ocean Park Hong Kong; 34l AA/B Bachman; 34/35t AA/B Bachman; 34/35c AA/B Bachman; 35t AA/B Bachman; 35cl AA/B Bachman; 35cr AA/B Bachman; 36l AA/D Henley; 36/37t AA/D Henley; 36/37c AA/D Henley; 37cl AA/D Henley; 37cr AA/D Henley; 38l AA/B Bachman; 38/39t AA/B Bachman; 38/39c AA/B Bachman; 39t AA/B Bachman; 39c Hong Kong Tourism Board; 40b AA/B Bachman; 41-42t AA/N Hicks; 41bl AA/B Bachman; 41br AA/A Kouprianoff; 42bl AA/B Bachman; 42br AA/N Hicks; 43t Hong Kong Tourism Board; 44t Hong Kong Tourism Board; 45t AA/N Hicks; 46t AA/B Bachman; 47t AA/B Bachman; 48t AA/B Bachman; 49t AA/B Bachman; 50t AA/B Bachman; 51 AA/B Bachman; 54tl AA/N Hicks; 54tc AA/D Henley 54tr AA/A Kouprianoff; 55tl AA/N Hicks; 55tr AA/B Bachman; 56tl AA/B Bachman; 56tc AA/B Bachman; 56tr AA/B Bachman; 57tl AA/B Bachman; 57tc AA/B Bachman; 57tr AA/B Bachman; 58tl AA/B Bachman; 58/59t AA/B Bachman; 59tr AA/B Bachman; 60t AA/B Bachman; 60cl AA/N Hicks; 60cr AA/D Henley; 61t AA/B Bachman; 61cl AA/B Bachman; 61cr AA/B Bachman; 62t AA/B Bachman; 62/63c Hong Kong Tourism Board; 63t AA/B Bachman; 64tl AA/B Bachman; 64tr AA/B Bachman; 65tl AA/B Bachman; 65tr AA/B Bachman; 66 AA/B Bachman; 67-69t Hong Kong Tourism Board; 67bl AA/D Henley; 67br AA/B Bachman; 68bl Hong Kong Tourism Board; 68br AA/B Bachman; 70t AA/B Bachman; 71t AA/B Bachman; 72 AA/B Bachman; 73t AA/B Bachman; 74t AA/B Bachman; 75t Hong Kong Tourism Board; 76t Hong Kong Tourism Board; 77 AA/B Bachman; 80t Hong Kong Wetland Park; 80cl Hong Kong Wetland Park; 80cr Hong Kong Wetland Park; 81t Hong Kong Wetland Park; 81cl Hong Kong Wetland Park; 81cr AA/B Bachman; 82l AA/B Bachman; 82/83t AA/B Bachman; 82/83c AA/B Bachman; 83t AA/B Bachman; 83cl AA/B Bachman; 83cr AA/B Bachman; 84tl AA/A Kouprianoff; 84tr AA/A Kouprianoff; 85-86t AA/B Bachman; 85bl Hong Kong Tourism Board; 85br AA/B Bachman; 86bl AA/A Kouprianoff; 86br Hong Kong Tourism Board; 87t AA/B Bachman; 88 AA/B Bachman; 89t AA/B Bachman; 89c Hong Kong Tourism Board; 90t AA/B Bachman; 91 AA/B Bachman; 94bl AA/B Bachman; 94tr AA/B Bachman; 94/95c Hong Kong Tourism Board; 95t AA/B Bachman; 95cl AA/B Bachman; 95cr AA/B Bachman; 96t © Disney; 96cl © Disney; 96cl © Disney; 97t © Disney; 97cl © Disney 97cr © Disney; 98l Hong Kong Tourism Board; 98tr AA/B Bachman; 98cr AA/B Bachman; 99t Hong Kong Tourism Board; 99cl AA/B Bachman; 99cr AA/B Bachman; 100-101t AA/B Bachman; 100b Hong Kong Tourism Board; 101bl © Nik Wheeler/Corbis; 101br © James Davis Photography/ Alamy; 102t AA/B Bachman; 103bl AA/I Morejohn; 103bl AA/I Morejohn; 103bc AA/A Kouprianoff; 103br AA; 104t AA/D Henley; 104bl AA/D Henley; 104br AA/B Bachman; 105 AA/B Bachman; 106t AA/B Bachman; 106c Photodisc; 107 AA/B Bachman; 108-112t AA/C Sawyer; 108tr AA/B Bachman; 108tcr Hong Kong Tourism Board; 108cr Hong Kong Tourism Board; 108br AA/B Bachman; 113 AA/B Bachman; 114-125t AA/B Bachman; 117bl Hong Kong Tourism Board; 120 MRI Bankers' Guide to Foreign Currency, Houston, USA; 122 AA/B Bachman; 124bl Hong Kong Tourism Board; 124br AA/B Bachman; 125bl AA/B Bachman; 125bc Hong Kong Tourism Board; 125br AA/D Henley

Every effort has been made to trace the copyright holders, and we apologise in advance for any accidental errors. We would be happy to apply the corrections in the following edition of this publication.